Experiences

READING LITERATURE

JOHN DENNIS

HEINLE & HEINLE PUBLISHERS

A Division of Wadsworth, Inc.
Boston, Massachusetts 02116

Library of Congress Cataloging-in-Publication Data

Dennis, John, 1920 –
  Experiences : reading literature.

  1. College readers. 2. English language – Text-books for foreign speakers.
3. Literature – Collections.
I. Title.
PE1122.D43   1987   428.6′4   86-19261

Sponsoring editor: James Brown
Production coordinator: Maeve A. Cullinane
Art research: Janice Miller
Cover design: Leslie Bartlett
Interior design: Carson Design
Compositor: Publication Services, Inc.
Printer: McNaughton & Gunn
Art and reading credits on page iv.

Printed in the U.S.A.   First printing: February 1987
63 21343   6 8 10 9 7 5

ISBN 0-8384-2819-3

CONTENTS

Credits

Readings:

Reflections on the Iguana / from OUT OF AFRICA by Isak Dinesen. Copyright 1937 by Random House, Inc. and renewed Copyright 1965 by Rungstedlundfonden. Reprinted by permission of Random House, Inc.

To Christ Our Lord / from WHAT A KINGDOM IT WAS by Galway Kinnell. Copyright © 1960 by Galway Kinnell. Reprinted by permission of Houghton Mifflin Company.

Reflections on the Death of a Porcupine / from PHOENIX II: *Uncollected, Unpublished, and Other Prose Works by D.H. Lawrence,* edited by Warren Roberts and Harry T. Moore. Copyright 1925 by the Centaur Press, renewed Copyright 1953 by Frieda Lawrence. Reprinted by permission of Viking Penguin Inc. Permission also granted by Laurence Pollinger Ltd. and the Estate of Mrs. Frieda Lawrence Ravagli.

Snake / from THE COMPLETE POEMS OF D.H. LAWRENCE, Collected and edited by Vivian de Sola Pinto and F. Warren Roberts. Copyright © 1964, 1971 by Angelo Ravagli and C.M. Weekly, Executors of The Estate of Frieda Lawrence Ravagli. Reprinted by permission of Viking Penguin Inc.

In the Tree House at Night / Copyright © 1981 by James Dickey. Reprinted from THE EARLY MOTION by permission of Wesleyan University Press.

The Parsley Garden / Copyright 1986 by the William Saroyan Foundation.

The Death of the Hired Man / from THE POETRY OF ROBERT FROST edited by Edward Connery Lathem. Copyright 1930, 1939, © 1969 by Holt, Rinehart and Winston. Copyright 1958 by Robert Frost. Copyright © 1967 by Lesley Frost Ballantine. Reprinted by permission of Holt, Rinehart and Winston, Publishers.

The Correspondence School Teacher Says Goodbye to His Students / from BODY RAGS by Galway Kinnell. Copyright © 1967 by Galway Kinnell. Reprinted by permission of Houghton Mifflin Company.

Mother and Son / from THE STORIES OF LIAM O'FLAHERTY. Reprinted by permission of Devin Adair Publishers.

Cress Delahanty: Winter / from CRESS DELAHANTY. Copyright 1953 by Jessamyn West. Reprinted by permission of Harcourt Brace Jovanovich, Inc. Also reprinted by permission of Russell & Volkening, Inc. as agents for the author. Copyright © 1946, renewed Copyright 1974 by Jessamyn West.

Cress Delahanty: Spring / from CRESS DELAHANTY. Copyright 1953 by Jessamyn West. Reprinted by permission of Harcourt Brace Jovanovich, Inc. Also reprinted by permission of Russell & Volkening, Inc. as agents for the author. Copyright © 1953 by Curtis Publishing, renewed Copyright 1981 by Jessamyn West.

Harlem / Copyright 1951 by Langston Hughes. Reprinted from SELECTED POEMS OF LANGSTON HUGHES, by permission of Alfred A. Knopf, Inc.

Feast / Reprinted by permission of South Dakota Review, Autumn, 1971.

Tularecito / from PASTURES OF HEAVEN by John Steinbeck. Copyright © 1932, 1960 by John Steinbeck. All rights reserved. Reprinted by permission of Viking Penguin Inc. Also reprinted by permission of Curtis Brown Ltd., London on behalf of the author's estate.

The Filipino and the Drunkard / Copyright 1986 by the William Saroyan Foundation.

Sam and the Rutabagas and *The Perfect Pill* / from the book THE PERFECT SOLUTION TO PRACTICALLY EVERYTHING by Arthur Hoppe, copyright © 1968 by Arthur Hoppe. Reprinted by permission of Doubleday & Company, Inc.

The Miser and *The Inheritance* / W.S. Merwin. "The Miser" and "The Inheritance" from HOUSES AND TRAVELLERS. Copyright © 1977 W.S. Merwin. Reprinted with the permission of Atheneum Publishers, Inc. and David Higham Associates Limited.

At the Public Library / Copyright 1986 by the William Saroyan Foundation.

Art:

Courtesy, Museum of Fine Arts, Boston: page 10 (*Winter Days,* ca. 1916/Aldro Hubbard/American, 1886–1972/Oil on canvas/Gift in Memory of Elizabeth Brown Barrett. 20.598); page 96 (*Painter's Honeymoon*/Leighton, Frederick, Lord/British, 1830–1896/Oil on canvas/32 ⅞ x 30 ¼ in. (83.5 x 76.8 cm.)/Charles H. Bayley Picture and Painting Fund. 1981.258; page 104 (*Boys in a Pasture*/Winslow Homer/American, 1836–1910/Oil on canvas/The Hayden Collection, 53.2552)

Janice Miller: pages 38 and 114

Courtesy of Boston Public Library, Print department: pages 48 (William Saroyan), 64 (Robert Frost) and 124 (Jessamyn West)

The J. Paul Getty Museum: page 78 (*Man with a Hoe,* Jean-Francois Millet)

Rafael Millan: page 88

Nicholas Muray: International Museum of Photography at George Eastman House: page 134 (Langston Hughes)

Alfred G. Simmer, photographer: Alaska Historical Society: page 140

National Maritime Museum: page 166

U.S. Department of Agriculture, Office of Governmental and Public Affairs: page 178

Johnnie Walker/THE PICTURE CUBE: page 186

David S. Strickler/THE PICTURE CUBE: page 192

Harvard Photo Lab/Jane Reed: page 199

Frank Siteman MCMLXXXII/THE PICTURE CUBE: page 210

A Note to Teachers

THE SELECTIONS

Experiences: *Reading Literature* is a collection of 22 pieces of literature, especially selected for upper intermediate and advanced learners of English as a Second or Foreign Language. It is equally appropriate for students studying literature in standard English courses. None of these selections has been "adapted" or edited. All of them have been glossed when items, idioms, or phrases seemed to present problems in comprehension for students at this level of achievement. There should be enough material in *Experiences* for one semester's work, or about 45 hours of classroom instruction.

All of the writers whose work is collected here are "good"; some of them are "great." But goodness or greatness wasn't the criterion for including them in *Experiences*. The criteria for selection were these.

Accessibility

Literature is commonly believed to be more difficult than non-literature (i.e., informative writing that might appear in the daily press as a report or feature article). Consequently, I searched for literature that could be used without adaptation (simplification) or editing (removing the "hard parts"). Naturally, some vocabulary needed glossing, and that was done whenever it was necessary or desirable.

Engagement

Experiences is a "reader," but reading literature has implications for the learner that go beyond skimming, scanning, and answering comprehension questions. Literature intends to entertain and to instruct in special ways. Unless writing can engage students by providing experiences that puzzle them, that draw them in, that make them feel and see, and that cause them to reflect, then two of the great benefits of reading — intellectual pleasure and emotional response — are missing.

If a poem or a prose piece engages students, we have an opportunity to teach them how to read literature. Once students learn how to read literature, they can continue to read it with some degree of satisfaction for the rest of their lives, beyond the classroom. As someone once remarked, "Man does not live by bread alone."

Consequences

When poetry and prose selections proved to be accessible and engaging, they had to meet another test: they had to contain linguistic resources and some kind of personal meaning—some means of identification—for a wide and varied audience of readers. The linguistic resources—the relationship I've called Structure and Style in *Experiences*—are those recurrent uses of structures and words that enable us to see the choices that the writer made in "putting the vision on the page." One consequence of this activity is the reader's realization that literature is not some mystical substance; it is a "verbal contraption," as W. H. Auden said, made of language used artfully. Not everyone can write literature, but most of us can learn to read it, once we get over the mistaken belief that it is somehow beyond our understanding.

One of the paradoxes of literature is that the experiences and people we read about are really quite different from our experiences and ourselves. Yet if the writer's craft and art are good enough to engage us, we identify with these strange places, times, people, and events, and they become familiar. We "own" them, and they become part of our "reality" and part of our lives. If the task of poetry, as one poet stated, is "to make the familiar strange," then the reader's task is to take the strange and make it familiar. We will probably never know how readers (or listeners) do this. Our task as teachers is to provide the experiences and conditions that allow this mysterious event to happen.

Reflection of Culture: Place and Time

The literature in *Experiences* is not limited to the contemporary world nor to America. Time ranges from the Renaissance to the present day. Places are as diverse as Africa, Italy, England, Ireland, and California. Since literature often grows out of specific places and times (real or imagined) and reflects the culture from which it emerges, students need to see these relationships as a "ground" for the writer's particular "configuration" or "schema." Consequently, the prereading material called Head Notes and Cultural Notes offer a kind of cultural setting for each selection in *Experiences*.

Topics

As I discovered the poetry and prose selections that were accessible, engaging, consequential, and culturally diverse for inclusion in *Experiences*, I also found ways of grouping them under topical headings. The use of topics or "themes" for a small group of readings is an old method whose value has been recently rediscovered. One of the first texts I used in university classes forty years ago was called *Patterns for Living* (Macmillan) by Caroline Shrodes and Justine van Gundy. They believed that students learned more effectively when discrete experiences were categorized under a semantic rubric that provided a meaningful and purposeful linkage for those varied readings. I have never doubted the wisdom of such an arrangement. Suzanne Griffin and I used it in *Reflections* (Newbury House), and it is reassuring to learn that current research in reading has discovered the value of topical organization in readers.

Topical organization means that sequence is not determined by level of difficulty. Some selections are more demanding than others and can be omitted, if necessary. The order in which the selections are used can be determined by the needs and interests of those using them.

DESIGN AND PROCEDURES

Head Notes

Every selection in *Experiences* is preceded by Head Notes; they offer simple biographical information to students. The Head Notes should be read, but they should not be confused with the experience of reading the material they precede, nor should students be tested for information from Head Notes.

Cultural Notes

As preparation for reading the poems and prose pieces in *Experiences*, Cultural Notes are usually of considerable importance. Students may read them silently, or the teacher may read them aloud. Oral questions and answers are desirable in either case, to "set the stage."

Strategies

In an ideal situation, the poetry and prose in *Experiences* should be presented orally by the teacher directly. Students would then read the texts as they listen to them. Having students read aloud is usually not a good procedure for several reasons: (a) Reading aloud is really a test of pronunciation rather than instruction in reading skill. (b) Students can read no faster than they can speak. (c) Reading aloud usually inhibits and embarrasses most students who are learning to speak and read English as a Second or Foreign Language. (d) It is not an efficient use of the limited amount of time available for instruction.

On the other hand, listening and reading are clearly related skills, just as speaking and writing are related. One of the tasks of reading is learning to understand the relationship between sounds and the symbols that represent them. Consequently, listening while one reads is a form of reinforcement and clarification. Furthermore, the rhymes and rhythms of poetry, for example, don't "come off the page." They need to be heard, especially when spelling obscures the presence of rhyme. Likewise, the emotional qualities contained in many of the selections in *Experiences* will be lost. Irony, sarcasm, anger, uncertainty, and tenderness frequently depend on "tone of voice" or "intonation." If these uses of language and feeling are not heard, they may not be perceived by students at all.

Ideally, then, students would listen and read more or less simultaneously. Before students would read the selection silently to themselves they would study the questions asked in Strategies. They may be able to answer some of the questions already, after listening and reading. If so, they should write down their answers or underline the appropriate sections of text where the answers may be found. Then students would reread the text, jotting down answers or marking the text, as they choose.

Of course, the point of this exercise is to give students instructions and directions for careful and critical reading. But notice that the analysis of the reading selection comes after students have had the first reading experience. The principle here is that the experience or "play" with literary material always precedes the analysis of it. Further, "informed reading" or "directed reading" as proposed in Strategies allows for an interplay between questions and answers as the student reads—not after the experience is over, as is the case with the typical lists of comprehension questions. The questions in Strategies are guides in the process of reading, not terminal tests.

When it is not possible or practical to observe the practice just described, students should read silently twice: the first time for the experience and the second time with the aid of the reading guides presented in Strategies. Although this is not an ideal teaching/learning situation, it is practicable and it will work. Finally, in either case, a few of the prose pieces in *Experiences* are rather long and may need to be divided for best results.

After the second reading, students should be encouraged to present their answers orally. When there is a difference of opinion, the teacher can take the students back to the text to look at the evidence. Questions of "fact" (information retrieval) will usually not present problems. Questions of inference or coming to judgment will present differences of interpretation. Such occasions will give both teachers and students valuable insights into how people read and think about what they read (or don't read, more likely). Discussions of this kind are apt to be lively and instructive.

Retelling

After students have completed the Strategies section orally, they will have an opportunity to retell their experience in writing. Retelling looks like a cloze test, but it isn't. Retelling combines a number of activities through its use of "gapped information":

Controlled writing

Information retrieval

Grammar: form-classes and inflections

Semantics: appropriate vocabulary

All of these matters are presented and recycled throughout Retelling. At the outset, students are given a great deal of context into which they will put words that are appropriate, grammatically and semantically. Students will probably depend heavily on information retrieval at this stage.

Subsequently, there is less context and there are more blanks. Students should be encouraged to use whatever grammar and vocabulary will work. That is, they should depend less on trying to find the "exact words" in the text, and instead, try to make sensible and well-formed sentences with what they "know."

Finally, near the end of *Experiences*, the Retelling section consists of a departure from the earlier exercises. Students are given careful instructions for writing mini-compositions of their own.

Retelling is an integrated solution to these common practices: (1) Write a composition about X in your own words. (2) Complete the following (discrete) exercises: (a) grammar; (b) vocabulary; (c) spelling; (d) punctuation and capitalization; (e) etc. Giving students the opportunity to "write a composition" without guidance is ill-advised. They choke on too much freedom. Discrete exercises that lack references to the reading experience students have had are of dubious value. Retelling remedies both of these difficulties. Students follow a rhetorical design which is reasonable. Context is always present. Grammar and semantics are combined rather than being artificially separated.

Retelling should probably be done in class, where the teacher can act as a facilitator, but it could be done for homework as well. Students could read their work aloud for in-class correction, or they could hand in their written responses as compositions copied and completed from the text. Perhaps oral work in the early part of the course could be shifted to written work to be handed in later in the course. This is a choice that depends on a good many variables.

It may be an overstatement to say that Retelling is the heart of the follow-up activities in *Experiences*. Yet there is a value in it that the other sections don't have. Retelling intends to show students how to present an experience in language other than that of the experience itself. We do this all the time when we account for a variety of events in our lives. That is, we all tell stories about what we did or what happened to us. In this sense, Retelling is a kind of model for that kind of activity. It is useful in the classroom, of course, but beyond the classroom it is the substance of our interactions with other people: an argument we had, an accident, a meal in a restaurant, or a movie we watched. The list is formidable. Learning how to tell stories well and accurately can be taught and learned. Retelling attempts to show students some ways of accomplishing that worthy goal.

Structure and Style

This section is the consequence of Joseph Conrad's dictum: "My task which I am trying to achieve is, by the power of the written word to make you hear, to make you feel — it is, before all, to make you see. That — and no more, and it is everything."

Because style is so complex, Structure and Style presents only those recurrent features, those persistent choices that writers make, for students to examine. These features of writing are often presented as Connections. This term is ambiguous. On one hand, it asks, How does the writer "connect" language to thoughts and feelings? On the other hand, it asks, How do you (reader) connect with this piece of writing? Such matters as parallelism, the uses of modifiers, the uses of rhetorical questions, the uses of various registers and authenticity of speech in defining character, and so on, are covered.

Students are often given examples of these recurrent features and then asked to discover additional ones in the text to understand how and how often the writer used them. Not why the writer used them, but how. We may infer why, but we can't know why. We can see how. Students are sometimes asked to "do violence" to a writer's work by deleting or substituting words or structures. Contrast is a valuable way to learn: What happens if/when . . . ? Students also have opportunities to try their hands at writing, say, their own figures of speech (metaphors or similes).

The purpose of Structure and Style is to make students conscious of "style as choice" and to let them see what happens when alternative ways of expressing thoughts and feelings are used. Language analysis and language play are thus combined. The activities in this section would probably best be done as homework, to be followed by questions and discussion in class.

Last Words

There are always aspects of a literary experience that do not yield gracefully to any kind of mechanical scrutiny. Sometimes they are big moral issues posed by a poem or a story. Sometimes they are ambiguities in the way a story or poem ends. Not infrequently, they are unanalyzable matters of feeling on the reader's part. Last Words attempts to question these matters without offering "the correct answer." There may not, in fact, be a correct answer. As one of my professors used to say, "We may never find the truth, but the search for it is awesome."

John Dennis
Professor of English
San Francisco State University

A Note to Students

One afternoon not long ago, a young man appeared in my office at the university. He introduced himself, sat down, and took out a pad of paper and a pen.

"I'm from the campus newspaper," he said. "We're making a survey of some of the professors in the university. We're asking all of you the same question. If you were going to live on an island for an indefinite period of time, who or what would you take with you?"

I smiled at him. "Have you read Defoe's *Robinson Crusoe*?" I asked.

"No, sir, I'm afraid not," he said. "I'm not an English major. I'm into journalism."

"Defoe was a journalist, too," I told him. "He made his living that way for about twenty-five years. But he is famous for his novel, *Robinson Crusoe*. And you've never heard of it?"

"No, sir, but I'm making a note of it. How do you spell that last name again?"

"C-r-u-s-o-e: Crusoe. I think you'd enjoy it. It's an adventure story about an Englishman who lives on an island for eighteen years. You can see why I thought of Robinson Crusoe when you asked your question."

"Yes, sir," the young man said. "But what about you, professor? I came to interview you." He repeated the question slowly. "Who—or what—would you take with you to this island?"

"Tell me about the island."

He looked at his notes. "Well, sir, it has everything you need to survive: animals, fish, fruit and vegetables, drinking water, and—" he turned the page—"stuff to build a house."

"I see. Other people?"

"No, sir. See, that's why we're asking who or what you'd take with you."

"Yes. How many people could I take along?"

"Oh, just one. Your wife, maybe. Are you married?"

"Yes, I am. But the who or what bothers me. If I take my wife, then . . ."

"Then," he interrupted, "you can only take things for survival: like a gun and bullets, clothes, matches, fishing line and hooks, tools, a knife and seeds. Going to take your wife with you, then?"

"That depends," I replied. "Can I take paper and pens and books and a musical instrument along with my wife?"

"No, sir. The rules are pretty clear about that. It's one *or* the other. . . . Sorry. I didn't make the rules, sir." He waited.

"Well," I said, "maybe I won't take this trip. What will happen if I don't go?"

The young man shrugged. "Nothing, I guess. I'll just say that you couldn't make up your mind. The paper will say that, too." He waited.

"Okay. I've got a class in ten minutes. I'll tell you what I'll do. Leave your name, and I'll write you a letter, answering your question. Fair enough?"

The young man sighed. "I guess so. But I'm supposed to learn how to take notes when I interview people. So, it's not the same if you write me a letter. Well, thank you anyway. Here's my name." He wrote *Phil Fuller*. "You can send it to the newspaper office. I spend a lot of time there."

We stood up. "Read *Robinson Crusoe*, Mr. Fuller." I said.

"Oh, sure," Phil Fuller replied. "Tell me the name of the author again. . . ."

The letter that I sent to Phil Fuller was never published. I missed the newspaper deadline for the results of the survey. The editor of the newspaper returned my letter with a polite note. She ended her note with this line: "I'd like to take one of your classes some day."

Instead of throwing the letter away I saved it. I thought that someone might find it interesting. You, for instance. In part, my letter to Mr. Fuller said this:

". . . I see that you are not going to offer me a well-furnished house. You offer me tools for survival. I don't think I'll need the gun and bullets. I've never owned a gun or used one in my entire life. A diet of fish, vegetables, and fruit will be quite satisfactory.

"My most difficult decision was to leave my wife at home. You and your readers may think that I've chosen a lonely life. In one way, I have. To leave a life of love and companionship and sharing behind is terribly hard. I cannot recommend it to others, and you may wonder why I have decided to live by myself in a natural world surrounded by sea.

"You have offered me unlimited books, paper, and writing instruments. I will be solitary, but not lonely. Readers and writers are always solitary, you see, but they are rarely lonely. They may live in isolation and in poorly furnished living quarters, but their minds are well-furnished. And with each new experience they read or write, they add companions, conversation, and knowledge to their lives. Huck Finn and Holden Caulfield* are my younger brothers. I went to university with Hamlet. Herzog** is my colleague. And

---

*The principal character in a novel, *The Catcher in the Rye*, by J. D. Salinger
**The principal character in a novel of the same name by Saul Bellow

there are dozens of others, characters and writers themselves, who have shaped my life and furnished my mind. Their experiences have become my experiences. Their lives are as real and mysterious to me as my own life.

"The Chinese have a saying: To understand a man you must know his memories. Reading literature is reading someone's memories. To read a poem, a story, an essay, a play is to touch another mind and spirit and to move with it: as we say, to learn the 'shape' of another person's mind and the 'sound' of another person's feelings. And so it is, then, that we learn the world through these experiences made of language for us by strangers who become as familiar to us as our neighbors.

"Of course, the island and the problem you present are both fictions, Mr. Fuller. To prepare myself, I think I'll read Robinson C-r-u-s-o-e again."

John Dennis
Professor of English
San Francisco State University

EXPERIENCES

READING LITERATURE

I
NATURE

1

REFLECTIONS ON THE IGUANA

Isak Dinesen

HEAD NOTES

Isak Dinesen (1885–1962) was the name used by the Danish Baroness Karen Blixen. After an unhappy marriage and divorce, she lived in Kenya, then British East Africa. She managed a coffee plantation there from 1914 until 1931. Her best-known book is *Out of Africa* (1937), a personal history. The following fragment appears in that book.

CULTURAL NOTES

Iguanas live in warm climates. They vary in length from six inches to six feet. As you can see in the picture, an iguana looks like a little dragon. But it is really slow and timid and quite harmless to humans. When people see an iguana for the first time, they are usually afraid, because this lizard looks ugly and fierce. Perhaps fear is one reason that people kill iguanas.

STRATEGIES

"Reflections on the Iguana" is about several matters. The most important one is the matter of life and death. It is also about the differences between black and white people. Finally, it is about the value of things.

Here are some questions to guide your reading of this prose fragment:

Why did Isak Dinesen find iguanas attractive?

Why does she kill an iguana?

What happens to the dead iguana?

When Isak Dinesen buys a beautiful bracelet, it looks ugly on her arm. Why?

Why does she remember the fish in the Zoological Museum?

What advice does she offer the European settlers of East Africa? Why?

Reflections on the Iguana

Isak Dinesen

1   In the *Reserve* I have sometimes come upon the Iguana, the big lizards, as they were sunning themselves upon a flat stone in a river-bed. They are not pretty in shape, but nothing can be imagined more beautiful than their colouring. They shine like a heap of precious stones or like a *pane* cut out of an old church window. When, as you approach, they *swish* away, there is a flash of *azure*, green and purple over the stones, the colour seems to be standing behind them in the air, like a *comet's luminous tail*.

2   Once I shot an Iguana. I thought that I should be able to make some pretty things from his skin. A strange thing happened then, that I have never afterwards forgotten. As I went up to him, where he was lying dead upon his stone, and actually while I was walking the few steps, he *faded* and grew pale, all colour died out of him as in one long sigh, and by the time that I touched him he was grey and dull like a lump of *concrete*. It was the live *impetuous* blood *pulsating* within the animal, which had *radiated out* all that *glow and splendour*. Now that the flame was put out, and the soul had flown, the Iguana was as dead as a sandbag.

3   Often since I have, in some sort, shot an Iguana, and I have remembered the one of the Reserve. Up at Meru I saw a young Native girl with a bracelet on, a leather strap two inches wide, and *embroidered* all over with very small *turquoise-coloured* beads which *varied* a little in colour and played in green, light blue and *ultramarine*. It was an extraordinarily live thing; it seemed to draw breath on her arm, so that I wanted it for myself, and made Farah buy it from her. No sooner had it come upon my own arm than it *gave*

Reserve—land used for special purposes
pane—piece of glass
swish—move with a brushing sound
azure—light blue
comet's luminous tail—fiery end of a shooting star
faded—lost color
concrete—cement; building material
impetuous—energetic
pulsating—beating
radiated out—spread out
glow and splendour—light and beauty
embroidered—decorated
turquoise-coloured—blue-green
varied—differed
ultramarine—deep blue

up the ghost. It was nothing now, a small, cheap, purchased article of finery. It had been the *play of colours*, the duet between the turquoise and the "nègre" — that *quick*, sweet, brownish black, like *peat* and black pottery, of the Native's skin, — that had created the life of the bracelet.

4   In the *Zoological Museum of Pietermaritzburg*, I have seen, in a stuffed deep-water fish in a *showcase*, the same combination of colouring, which there had survived death; it made me wonder what life can well be like, on the bottom of the sea, to send up something so live and airy. I stood in Meru and looked at my pale hand and at the dead bracelet, it was as if an injustice had been done to a noble thing, as if truth had been *suppressed*. So sad did it seem that I remembered the saying of the hero in a book that I had read as a child: "I have *conquered* them all, but I am standing amongst graves."

5   In a foreign country and with foreign *species* of life one should *take measures* to find out whether things will be keeping their value when dead. To the settlers of East Africa I give the advice: "For the sake of your own eyes and heart, shoot not the Iguana."

RETELLING

The _____ of the iguana, Isak Dinesen tells us, is

_____, but its _____ is beautiful. The

_____ of the iguana's skin remind her of

_____, or of a _____ tail, because they

all _____.

---

gave up the ghost — died
play of colours — shift and change of colors
quick — alive
peat — earth; dark-brown
Zoological Museum of Pietermaritzburg — animal museum in Denmark
showcase — a cabinet made of glass
suppressed — held back; not shown
conquered — beaten; overcome
species — kinds, types
take measures — try

After _____ an iguana, she _____

something that she never _____. The live iguana

was _____ and lost all of its _____.

Isak Dinesen had a similar _____ when she

bought a _____ from a Native girl. When Isak

Dinesen put it on her _____ arm, the colors

_____, and it looked _____.

Isak Dinesen discovered the value of _____ things

and _____ things in a _____ country. Her

advice to European _____ in East Africa is never to

_____ the _____.

STRUCTURE AND STYLE

Associations: Nouns and Verbs

1. Isak Dinesen puts nouns and verbs together in unusual ways. Look at these verbs and think of nouns that we usually find before or after them.

   shine   swish
   standing   come upon
   faded   flown
   died   played
   grew   draw

2. Now look at these same verbs in Isak Dinesen's writing. What are the nouns that you find before or after them? Write them down with the verbs.

3. The difference between the lists in exercises 1 and 2 is very important. One is a list of ordinary pairs of nouns and verbs. We call them *literal* meanings. The other is a list of unusual pairs. We call them *figurative* meanings. Good writers learn to use both kinds of meanings.

Images: Similes and Metaphors

1. Isak Dinesen makes *images* in her writing in two ways: she uses comparisons and she makes words come together in imaginative ways.

   Similes are comparisons of two unlike things that use the words *as, as* _____ *as, like* to make images. *Metaphors* are words associated with each other in unusual ways to create images or *suggest* a comparison.

   Here are some examples taken from the text. Study them and then mark them as S (simile) or M (metaphor).

   a. (Iguanas) shine like a heap of precious stones

   b. the color seems to be standing behind them in the air

   c. like a comet's luminous tail

   d. (the iguana) faded

   e. he was grey and dull like a lump of concrete

   f. the soul had flown

   g. the Iguana was as dead as a sandbag

   h. (beads) played in green, light blue, and ultramarine

   i. the (bracelet) seemed to draw breath on her arm

   j. It had been . . . the duet between the turquoise and the nègre

   k. (skin) like peat and black pottery

2. Try making some images of your own. Here are some *similes* for you to complete.

   a. Her skin was as cold as _____.

   b. Her laughter sounded like _____.

   c. Your breath smells like _____.

   d. The cat moved as _____ as _____.

   e. Her touch was as light as _____.

   Can you think of others? Write them down.

LAST WORDS

In "Reflections on the Iguana" Isak Dinesen contrasts life and death. Make two lists: one that contains words, phrases, and sentences associated with life and a second that contains words, phrases, and sentences associated with death.

After you have made your lists and compared them, try to answer this question: Is Isak Dinesen writing for life or death? Why do you think so?

2
TO CHRIST
OUR LORD

Galway Kinnell

HEAD NOTES

Galway Kinnell (1927–), a native of Rhode Island, is considered one of the best modern American poets. He is often compared to Walt Whitman, a famous poet of the nineteenth century who described the heart and mind of the American people. Kinnell writes about experiences shared by all people. He is a poet of the twentieth-century American scene. He speaks of darkness and sadness, criminals, poor people, and crowded cities. He frequently uses words that make us think about fire and death. In 1982 he received the Pulitzer Prize and the American Book Award for Poetry.

CULTURAL NOTES

On holidays like Thanksgiving and Christmas, many Christians give thanks to God before they eat their holiday meal. This practice is called "saying grace." "Grace" is a prayer or a blessing, which often ends with these words: "We ask this in the name of Christ our Lord."

The food at the holiday table is plentiful, and it usually includes a turkey or a goose. Most people buy their holiday food in stores. But in some parts of the country, stores are far away. People in those lonely places still hunt for their food. They kill wild birds and animals in order to survive.

In the last century, people did not have gas or electricity for heat and light. They used stoves that burned wood, or they cooked over the coals of an open fire. They lighted their houses with oil lamps and candles. On some isolated farms, these old practices continue.

STRATEGIES

This is the first poem that you will read in this book. One way to recognize a poem is to look at its shape. Poems are placed on a page in a certain form. Their lines follow each other vertically. The lines are not necessarily complete sentences. Sometimes the last word in a line will "rhyme" — have the same sound — with the last word in the line before it: said/dead; pleased/seized; run/done. As you can see, words spelled differently may have the same sound. Poems may contain punctuation — commas, semicolons and periods — or they may not.

To make sense out of a poem, you must first decide how the lines connect with each other. Let's look at the first stanza (a division of a poem; in this case, a group of five lines) of "To Christ Our Lord." If you come to a complete stop—a period—at the end of lines 1, 2, and 3, the poem will be understandable. But what happens if you come to a complete stop at the end of line 4? Line 5 won't make sense. Lines 4 and 5 must connect: "a woman basted/ A bird . . .".

Another kind of connection is important. Look at "Hunting" in line 3. Who or what is hunting? The answer is in line 2: "wolves." You must go back to line 2 in order to make the connection. Sometimes the words that work together are next to each other: "elk living and frozen" and "A bird spread over coals." But they can be in reverse order, too: "wolves . . . lightfooted" means "light-footed wolves."

"To Christ Our Lord" tells a simple story. A boy kills a bird on Christmas Day. A woman, probably his mother, cooks it. Someone, perhaps his father, says grace and thanks God for this food: the bird a boy killed. The boy eats the bird and wonders why he killed it.

But the poem is about more than these events on Christmas Day. The thoughts and feelings of the boy—his "wonder" and his questions—puzzle him. He doesn't talk to others. He asks himself these difficult questions. And the poet, in turn, asks us, the readers, to share the boy's thoughts and feelings.

As you read "To Christ Our Lord," here are some questions to help you understand this poem:

Stanza 1

What is happening outside?

How do wolves walk on the snow?

What is happening inside?

Stanza 2

If snow had covered the windows and blocked the outside light, how can the people inside the house see what they are eating?

What does "being long-winded" connect with?

Someone killed the bird. Why does the boy ask: "Is it fitting to eat this creature killed on the wing?"

Stanza 3

The source of the boy's question appears in this stanza. How did he kill the bird?

What does "climbing out/ Alone . . ." connect with?

Is it snowing?

Why do you think the "fallen snow (is) swirling?"

What is the subject of "Heard . . . , Watched . . . , and fished . . . ?"

Stanza 4

What "stirred his love?"

Why had he "not wanted to shoot?"

What does "Famishing" connect with?

Why does he wonder "could he fire?"

Stanza 5

Who thinks that his act is "wicked?"

How does the grace "praise" his act?

Is he hungry?

To what or to whom did he "surrender?"

Stanza 6

Does he return to the scene of his "wicked act?" When?

What is his question now?

What is the weather like now?

Is there an answer to his question?

"The Swan" is the constellation of stars called *Cygnus* (Swan). It appears over the North Pole, in the form of a cross. What is a "pattern?" What does a "mirror" do?

Does the poem tell us that human beings are controlled by the stars?

To Christ Our Lord

Galway Kinnell

1 The legs of the *elk punctured* the snow's crust
2 And wolves floated lightfooted on the land
3 Hunting Christmas elk living and frozen;
4 Inside snow melted in a *basin*, and a woman *basted*
5 A bird spread over coals by its wings and head.

6 Snow had *sealed* the windows; candles lit
7 The Christmas meal. The Christmas grace *chilled*
8 The cooked bird, being *long-winded* and the room cold.
9 During the words a boy thought, is it *fitting*
10 To eat this creature killed *on the wing*?

11 He had killed it himself, climbing out
12 Alone on *snowshoes* in the Christmas dawn,
13 The fallen snow *swirling* and the snowfall gone,
14 Heard its throat scream as the gunshot scattered,
15 Watched it drop, and *fished* from the snow the dead.

---

elk – a large deer
punctured – pierced
basin – a large bowl
basted – moistened with liquid
sealed – covered
chilled – made cold
long-winded – long in speaking
fitting – right; appropriate
on the wing – while flying
snowshoes – wooden shoes used for walking on snow
swirling – blowing and twisting
fished – pulled out

16 He had not wanted to shoot. The sound
17 Of wings beating into the *hushed* air
18 Had *stirred his love*, and his fingers
19 Froze in his gloves, and he wondered,
20 *Famishing*, could he fire? Then he fired.

21 Now the grace praised his *wicked* act. At its end
22 The bird on the plate
23 Stared at his *stricken* appetite.
24 There had been nothing to do but *surrender*,
25 To kill and to eat; he ate as he had killed, with wonder.

26 At night on snowshoes on the *drifting* field
27 He wondered again, for whom had love stirred?
28 The stars *glittered* on the snow and nothing answered.
29 Then *the Swan* spread her wings, cross of the cold north,
30 The pattern and mirror of the acts of earth.

RETELLING

Early on _____ _____, a boy went out

on _____. He carried a _____. He heard

the sound of _____ in the air, and he

_____. He _____ a _____. A

woman _____ the _____ for Christmas

---

hushed — quiet
stirred his love — made him feel love
famishing — suffering, starving
wicked — evil
stricken — injured or almost lost
surrender — give (oneself) up
drifting — windy and snowy
glittered — shone brightly
swan — a white, long-necked graceful bird; the Swan, however, is a
   constellation of stars

_____. Someone said _____, and the

boy _____ why he had _____ the

_____. He had not _____ to

_____. He felt _____ stir inside him. But

he _____ his _____, anyway. When he

_____ the _____ on his plate he

_____ it with _____. There was

_____ he could do but _____. Later, he

_____ to the snow field and _____

again. For whom had _____ _____? The

answer to his question was _____. The

_____ above him _____ in the sky.

STRUCTURE AND STYLE

Connections: A. Verbs Modifying Nouns

Like Isak Dinesen, Galway Kinnell connects nouns and pronouns with verbs in interesting ways. In his poem, Kinnell makes verbs modify nouns. He uses this so often that we can call it a *pattern*. Sometimes the form is verb + *-ing* + noun; sometimes it is verb + *-ed* or *-en* + noun. The verb may come before or after the noun (or pronoun) it modifies.

Beginning with stanza 1, line 2, we find "wolves . . . lightfooted . . .". Go through the poem one line at a time and write down all of the verb-noun modifications you can find.

B. Synonyms

One way to understand the power of words is to replace them with "synonyms"—words that "have the same meaning." Here is a list of "synonyms" for some of the verbs in "To Christ Our Lord."

Match them with the verbs in the poem. Then try to answer this question: What happens to the poem if these synonyms replace the verbs that Kinnell used? Is it the same poem?

pierced	agitated
walked	starving
cooked	lost
covered	give up
shot	considered
moving	shone
pulled out	

LAST WORDS

Many people feel that a poem is not a poem unless it has words that rhyme at the ends of lines. Rhyming means that words sound alike (see Strategies, p. 11).

Can you find in this poem pairs of words at the ends of lines that have similar sounds? If so, where do you find these lines in the stanzas of the poem?

Is rhyming the most important element in the structure of Kinnell's poem or not?

3
REFLECTIONS ON THE DEATH OF A PORCUPINE

D. H. Lawrence

HEAD NOTES

David Herbert Lawrence (1885–1931), British writer, died at the age of forty-five. During his brief life, he wrote poetry, short stories, novels, journals of his travels, plays, and literary criticism. Lawrence's most famous novel is *Lady Chatterley's Lover*. Because of the love scenes in this novel, the English government would not allow it to be sold for many years. The government's action angered Lawrence, and he spent a good deal of time living in other countries. He lived in the United States for a period of time. He chose to live in New Mexico. The climate there was good for his health; he suffered from lung disease, which eventually caused his death.

CULTURAL NOTES

"Reflections on the Death of a Porcupine" is from work Lawrence wrote during his New Mexico experience. "Madame" is his wife. Lawrence and Madame are living on a small ranch, and Lawrence thinks of himself as a rancher at this time in his life. Ranching is a new experience for the Lawrences. They are not prepared for its difficulties and dangers.

Lawrence and his wife thought that porcupines were dangerous. It is true that porcupines can injure other animals. Porcupines (Latin *porcus*, pig + *spina*, spine) carry spines or quills that pierce the flesh of anything that gets too close. Lawrence's dog was injured by a porcupine, and Lawrence came to hate porcupines. Porcupines don't attack people; people attack porcupines.

STRATEGIES

Like the boy in Kinnell's poem, Lawrence "had not wanted to shoot." But the boy was "stirred by love;" Lawrence tells his readers "And again I disliked him." (Lawrence first disliked the porcupine because it had injured his dog.)

⟋ Why does he dislike it "again?"

The rest of Lawrence's narrative is an argument for his right to kill "things." Here are some questions to guide your reading of "Reflections on the Death of a Porcupine:"

When Lawrence asks Madame, his wife, "Should one kill him?", how does she answer and what does she say?

Lawrence tells us that "something slowly hardens in a man's soul." What do you think he means?

Why is Lawrence an unsuccessful hunter?

When Lawrence again questions his wife—"Does it seem mean?"—how does she answer and what does she say?

Lawrence tells himself: "One must kill." Why?

Lawrence tells us that he will kill another porcupine. Why?

The rest of Lawrence's writing is an argument: man must fight for food against "the lower orders of life." What are these lower orders of life?

What connection do you find between Lawrence's action (killing a porcupine) and his argument (man's fight against animals)?

Reflections on the Death of a Porcupine

D. H. Lawrence

1   And then the present moon came, and again the night was clear. But in the *interval* there had been heavy thunder-rains, the ditch was running with bright water across the field, and the night, so fair, had not the terrific, mirror-like *brilliancy*, *touched with terror*, so *startling* bright, of the moon in the last days of June.

2   We were alone on the ranch. Madame went out into the clear night, just before *retiring*. The stream ran in a cord of silver across the field, in the straight line where I had taken the irrigation ditch. The pine tree in front of the house threw a black shadow. The mountain slope came down to the fence, wild and *alert*.

3   "Come!" said she excitedly. "There is a big porcupine drinking at the ditch. I thought at first it was a bear."

---

interval—period of time; several days
brilliancy—brightness
touched with terror—rather frightening
startling—surprisingly
retiring—going to bed
alert—watchful

4   When I got out he had gone. But among the grasses and the coming wild sunflowers, under the moon, I saw his greyish *halo*, like a *pallid* living bush, moving over the field, in the distance, in the moonlit *clair-obscur*.

5   We got through the fence, and following, soon *caught him up*. There he *lumbered*, with his white spoon-tail *spiked with bristles*, steering behind almost as if he were moving backwards, and this was his head. His long, long hairs above the quills *quivering* with a dim grey gleam, like a bush.

6   And again I disliked him.

7   "Should one kill him?"

8   She hesitated. Then with a sort of *disgust*:

9   "Yes!"

10   I went back to the house, and got the little twenty-two rifle. Now never in my life had I shot at any live thing: I never wanted to. I always felt guns very *repugnant*, *sinister*, *mean*. With difficulty I had fired once or twice at a target: but *resented* doing even so much. Other people could shoot if they wanted to. Myself, individually, it was repugnant to me even to try.

11   But something slowly hardens in a man's soul. And I knew now, it had hardened in mine. I found the gun, and with rather trembling hands, got it loaded. Then I pulled back the trigger and followed the porcupine. It was still lumbering through the grass. Coming near, I *aimed*.

12   The trigger stuck. I pressed the little *catch* with a safety-pin I found in my pocket, and released the trigger. Then we followed the porcupine. He was still lumbering towards the trees. I went sideways on, stood quite near to him, and fired, in the clear-dark of the moonlight.

---

halo — circle of light around him
pallid — pale; lacking color
clair-obscur — light and dark; shadowy
caught him up — came to where he was
lumbered — walked heavily
spiked with bristles — quills standing up
quivering — shaking
disgust — great dislike
repugnant, sinister, mean — disgusting, revolting, of low quality
resented — greatly disliked
aimed — pointed (the gun)
catch — piece of metal that holds the trigger (a safety catch)

13   And as usual I aimed too high. He turned, went *scuttling* back whence he had come.

14   I got another *shell* in place, and followed. This time I fired full into the mound of his round back, below the glistening grey halo. He seemed to stumble on to his hidden nose, and *struggled a few strides*, ducking his head under like a *hedgehog*.

15   "He's not dead yet! Oh, fire again!" cried Madame.

16   I fired, but the gun was empty.

17   So I ran quickly, for a *cedar pole*. The porcupine was lying still, with *subsiding* halo. He *stirred faintly*. So I turned him and hit him hard over the nose; or where, in the dark, his nose should have been. And it was done. He was dead.

18   And in the moonlight, I looked down on the first creature I had ever shot.

19   "Does it seem mean?" I asked aloud, doubtful.

20   Again Madame hesitated. Then: "No!" she said resentfully.

21   And I felt she was right. Things like the porcupine, one must be able to shoot them, if they get in one's way.

22   One must be able to shoot. I, myself, must be able to shoot, and to kill.

23   For me, this is a *volte-face*. I have always preferred to walk round my porcupine, rather than kill it.

24   Now, I know it's not good walking round. One must kill.

25   I buried him in the *adobe* hole. But some animal dug down and ate him; for two days later, there lay the spines and bones spread out, with the long skeletons of the porcupine-hands.

---

scuttling — running quickly
shell — bullet
struggled a few strides — moved a few feet with difficulty
hedgehog — an animal that can roll itself up
cedar pole — a long wooden stick
subsiding — fading
stirred faintly — moved a little bit
volte-face — a complete change
adobe — heavy clay soil

27 The only nice thing about him—or her, for I believe it was a female, by the *dugs* on her belly—were the feet. They were like longish, alert black hands, paw-hands. That is why a porcupine's tracks in the snow look almost as if a child had gone by, leaving naked little human foot-prints, like a little boy.

28 So, he is gone: or she is gone. But there is another one, bigger and blacker-looking, among the west *timber*. That too is to be shot. It is part of the business of ranching: even when it's only a little *half-abandoned* ranch like this one.

29 Wherever man *establishes* himself, upon the earth, he has to fight for his place, against the *lower orders* of life. Food, the basis of existence, has to be fought for even by the most *idyllic* of farmers. You plant, and you protect your growing crop with a gun. Food, food, how strangely it relates man with the animal and vegetable world! How important it is! And how fierce is the fight that goes on around it.

30 The same when one skins a rabbit, and takes out the inside, one realizes what an enormous part of the animal, comparatively, is intestinal, what a big part of him is just for food-apparatus; for living on other organisms.

31 And when one watches the horses in the big field, their noses to the ground, bite-bite-biting at the grass, and stepping absorbedly on, and bite-bite-biting without ever lifting their noses, *cropping off* the grass, the young shoots of alfalfa, the dandelions, with a *blind, relentless, unwearied persistence*, one's whole life pauses. One suddenly realizes again how all creatures *devour*, and must devour the lower forms of life.

32 So *Susan*, swinging across the field, snatches off the tops of the little wild sunflowers as if she were *mowing*. And down they go, down her black throat. And when she stands in her cowy *oblivion* chewing her *cud*, with her

---

dugs—female breasts
timber—trees
half-abandoned—poorly maintained
establishes—settles
lower orders—lower classes or kinds
idyllic—peaceful
cropping off—leaving almost nothing
blind, relentless, unwearied persistence—thoughtless, hard, energetic
    continuation
devour—eat greedily
Susan—Lawrence's cow
mowing—cutting with a machine
oblivion—lack of memory
cud—food chewed by cows

lower jaw swinging peacefully, and I am milking her, suddenly the *camomiley* smell of her breath, as she glances round with *glaring*, smoke-blue eyes, makes me realize it is the sunflowers that are her ball of cud. Sunflowers! And they will go to making her *glistening* black hide, and the thick cream on her milk.

33   And the chickens, when they see a great black beetle, that the Mexicans call a *toro*, floating past, they are after it in a rush. And if it settles, instantly the brown hen stabs it with her beak. It is a great beetle two or three inches long: but in a second it is in the *crop* of the chicken. Gone!

RETELLING

At the _____ of _____ "Reflections on

the Death of a Porcupine," D. H. Lawrence and

_____ were living on a _____ in

_____. _____, Lawrence's wife, sees a

_____ and calls her _____. Lawrence

asks his wife if he should _____ the animal. When

_____ says _____, Lawrence

_____ to the house and gets a small

_____. He has never _____ any

_____ thing in his entire _____. Guns

are _____ to him. Nevertheless, he

_____ the porcupine, but the _____

---

camomiley—smelling of the herb, camomile
glaring—staring angrily
glistening—shining
toro—bull (Spanish)
crop—like a stomach (in birds only)

doesn't _____ it. Lawrence has to finish the job with

a _____ _____.

   This experience _____ Lawrence's attitude toward

_____ animals. He used to _____ guns.

Now he says, " One must _____." There is another

_____ on his property. Lawrence says that he

_____ _____ that one, too.

   Lawrence now _____ that man must

_____ against the _____

_____ of life, because every living creature needs

_____. A man must _____ his

_____ with a _____. Every creature

_____ the lower _____ of

_____. _____ and _____ eat

grass and flowers. _____ eat _____. This

constant struggle for _____ relates man to the

_____ and _____ world.

STRUCTURE AND STYLE

Connections: A. Connectors

Little words like *and*, *but*, and *so* are called "structure words."
They do not have meaning in themselves as the words *house*, *gun*,
and *animal* have meaning. Yet these little "connectors" can help
to make a writer's style: the way that the writer says things to a
reader.

1. Look at Lawrence's narrative once again. Check the number of
   sentences that begin with *and*, *but*, and *so*. How many did you
   find?

2. Remove these words from the beginning of each of the sentences. Do the meanings of those sentences change? Does the removal of *and*, *but*, and *so* make any difference at all? If you think so, how would you describe this difference?

3. Do you think that Lawrence's style depends in an important way on his use of these little connectors? Why or why not?

B. Verb + *-ing* forms

Lawrence often uses verb + *-ing* forms in his narrative. Sometimes they are used as verbs. Sometimes they are used as *modifiers* of nouns or pronouns (participles).

1. It may be possible to reconstruct a large part of the narrative by using the verb + *-ing* forms and connecting them with nouns and pronouns.

   Let's try this. Start at the beginning of the narrative. Find the noun or pronoun that connects with the verb + *-ing* form in the list.

   _____ running

   startling (bright) _____

   _____ retiring

   _____ drinking

   coming _____

   living _____

   _____ moving

   _____ following

   _____ steering

   _____ moving (backwards)

   _____ quivering

   trembling _____

   _____ lumbering

   _____ scuttling

   glistening _____

_____ ducking (his head)

_____ lying (still)

2. Which sections of the narrative are missing from the preceding list? How are verbs used in those sections of the narrative?

LAST WORDS

"Reflections on the Death of a Porcupine" is composed of two parts: a narrative and an argument.

Where does the narrative end? Why do you think so?

Where does the argument begin?

What change do you find in the use of *pronouns*, when you go from the narrative to the argument?

Which of the two parts, the narrative or the argument, do you prefer? Why?

4
SNAKE

D. H. Lawrence

HEAD NOTES

See page 19.

CULTURAL NOTES

D. H. Lawrence was living in Taormina, Sicily, when he wrote "Snake," one of his best-known poems. Lawrence tells us that it is July; it is very hot; and Mt. Etna, Sicily's live volcano, is smoking.

Lawrence refers to his "accursed human education." He means that he was taught to hate snakes and to think of animals as inferior to human beings. It was this education that made it possible for Lawrence to kill the porcupine. In "Snake," he doubts the value of that education, even though he is afraid of this poisonous snake.

Lawrence also refers to the "albatross." This large seabird is a symbol of good luck to sailors. In a famous poem called "The Rime of the Ancient Mariner" by S. T. Coleridge, a sailor shoots and kills an albatross. Forever afterward, the sailor suffers from guilt and shame for his wicked act.

Lawrence's snake is more than a snake. It is sometimes like a person; sometimes like a god (Pluto) from the underworld. We see the snake. We come to know the poet.

STRATEGIES

There are two conflicts in this poem. The first conflict is man against beast. Both want water from the same place on a hot day. The second conflict is between the two voices within the man's (Lawrence's) mind. One voice admires the beauty of the snake. The other voice says, "If you were not afraid, you would kill him!"

As you read "Snake," let these questions guide you:

Why does the man decide to wait for water?

Which images in the poem express the snake's appearance?

In which lines does the man express his admiration for the snake?

At what point in the poem does the snake become more than a snake?

Why doesn't the man kill the snake?

Why does the man throw the log at the snake?

How does the man feel after throwing the log? Why?

Why does he want the snake to return?

Snake

D. H. Lawrence

1 A snake came to my *water-trough*
2 On a hot, hot day, and I in pajamas for the heat,
3 To drink there.

4 In the deep, strange-scented shade of the great dark carob-tree
5 I came down the steps with my pitcher
6 And must wait, must stand and wait, for there he was at the trough before
   me.

7 He reached down from a *fissure* in the earth-wall in the *gloom*
8 And trailed his yellow-brown *slackness* soft-bellied down, over the edge of
   the stone trough
9 And rested his throat upon the stone bottom,
10 And where the water had dripped from the tap, in a small clearness,
11 He sipped with his straight mouth,
12 Softly drank through his straight gums, into his slack long body,
13 Silently.

14 Someone was before me at my water-trough,
15 And I, like a second comer, waiting.

---

water-trough—a large container for water
fissure—a crack; an opening
gloom—darkness
slackness—looseness

16 He lifted his head from his drinking, as cattle do,

17 And looked at me vaguely, as drinking cattle do,

18 And *flickered* his *two-forked tongue* from his lips, and *mused* a moment,

19 And stooped and drank a little more,

20 Being earth-brown, earth-golden from the burning *bowels* of the earth

21 On the day of Sicilian July, with Etna smoking.

22 The voice of my education said to me

23 He must be killed,

24 For in Sicily the black, black snakes are innocent, the gold are *venomous*.

25 And voices in me said, If you were a man

26 You would take a stick and break him now, and *finish him off*.

27 But must I *confess* how I liked him,

28 How glad I was he had come like a guest in quiet, to drink at my
      water-trough

29 And depart peaceful, *pacified*, and thankless,

30 Into the burning bowels of this earth?

31 Was it *cowardice*, that I dared not kill him?

32 Was it *perversity*, that I *longed* to talk to him?

33 Was it *humility*, to feel so honored?

34 I felt so honored.

35 And yet those voices:

36 If you were not afraid, you would kill him!

---

flickered — moved in and out quickly
two-forked tongue — split at the tip
mused — thought
bowels — interior
venomous — poisonous
finish him off — kill him
confess — admit; tell the truth
pacified — calmed
cowardice — lack of courage
perversity — wrong behavior
longed — wanted very much
humility — lack of pride; modesty

37 And truly I was afraid, I was most afraid,
38 But even so, honored still more
39 That he should seek my *hospitality*
40 From out the dark door of the secret earth.

41 He drank enough
42 And lifted his head, dreamily, as one who has drunken,
43 And flickered his tongue like a *forked night* on the air, so black,
44 Seeming to lick his lips,
45 And looked around like a god, unseeing, into the air,
46 And slowly turned his head,
47 And slowly, very slowly, as if *thrice adream*,
48 Proceeded to draw his slow length curving round
49 And climb again the broken bank of my wall-face.

50 And as he put his head into that dreadful hole,
51 And as he slowly drew up, snake-easing his shoulders, and entered farther,
52 A sort of horror, a sort of *protest* against his withdrawing into that *horrid* black hole,
53 *Deliberately* going into the blackness, and slowly drawing himself after,
54 Overcame me now his back was turned.

55 I looked round, I put down my pitcher,
56 I picked up a clumsy log
57 And threw it at the water-trough with a *clatter*.

---

hospitality—generous welcome
forked night—lightning
thrice adream—deeply dreaming; nearly asleep
protest—objection; complaint
horrid—disgusting; ugly
deliberately—slowly and carefully
clatter—loud noise

58 I think it did not hit him,

59 But suddenly that part of him that was left behind *convulsed* in undignified
    haste

60 *Writhed* like lightning, and was gone

61 Into the black hole, the earth-lipped fissure in the wall-front,

62 At which, in the *intense* still noon, I stared with *fascination*.

63 And immediately I regretted it.

64 I thought how *paltry*, how *vulgar*, what a mean act!

65 I despised myself and the voices of my *accursed* human education.

66 And I thought of the *albatross*

67 And I wished he would come back, my snake.

68 For he seemed to me again like a king,

69 Like a king *in exile*, uncrowned in the underworld,

70 Now due to be crowned again.

71 And so, I missed my chance with one of the lords

72 Of life.

73 And I have something to *expiate*;

74 A *pettiness*.

---

convulsed — shook
writhed — twisted quickly
intense — very hot
fascination — wonder
paltry — low
vulgar — crude; offensive; lacking in understanding
accursed — evil; morally wrong
albatross — large seabird
in exile — forced to live outside one's country
expiate — get rid of
pettiness — a smallness of mind and spirit

RETELLING

In _____, there are two kinds

of _____: _____ snakes are

_____, but _____ snakes are

_____. And the snake in this poem is described as

_____ _____ because it lives in the

_____ of the _____. It

_____ from a _____ _____

while the man _____. As he _____ there,

the man has a _____ inside himself. Should he

_____ the snake, as his _____ taught

him? Or should he _____ the beauty of the snake?

He feels _____ by the snake's visit.

The man compares the snake first to a _____

being and then to a _____ from the

_____.

After the snake finishes _____, it begins to

_____ back into the _____ from which it

_____. The man _____ a

_____ at it, and the snake _____ quickly.

Afterwards, the man _____ his action. He

_____ himself. He _____ that the snake

would _____, because it seems to be a

_____ in _____. The man blames his

_____ for his _____ act.

STRUCTURE AND STYLE

Connections: Personification

In Lawrence's prose piece (pp. 20–24), animals are called "things" of a "lower order." In "Snake" Lawrence turns an animal into a human being. Lawrence does this with language, not with magic.

1. Read the poem again and write down every human characteristic Lawrence uses to describe the snake. Sometimes Lawrence uses nouns to personify the snake; other times he uses verbs or parts of sentences.

2. Now let's turn it around. Suppose you wanted to describe a human being as if he or she were a snake. Which characteristics of a snake would you use to do this? Think about shape; think about the way snakes move; think about eyes, tongue, and body temperature; think about the sound that snakes make with their mouths.

3. Once again, we find Lawrence using *and, and as, and so, but,* and *for* to begin lines of poetry. Remove these connectors. (Sometimes you will have to replace them with a pronoun to make sense.) What happens to the rhythm and movement of the poem when you remove these words? Do the connectors give meaning or style to Lawrence's poem?

LAST WORDS

"Snake" is a contrast between the beauty of an animal and the meanness of a human being. Snakes are usually described as ugly, dangerous, and frightening. How does Lawrence describe "my snake" to make it seem beautiful? How does Lawrence describe his own meanness?

5

IN THE
TREE
HOUSE
AT
NIGHT

James Dickey

HEAD NOTES

Poet, novelist, and critic James Dickey (1923–) was born in Atlanta, Georgia. He is a storyteller who is fascinated with the use of power and violence between men. He began writing poetry when he was twenty-four years old. His first poem was about football players. He has been an advertising executive, an athlete, and a fighter pilot. He is best known for his novel, *Deliverance*, which was made into a very popular movie. He wrote the screen play after spending eight years on the novel. Dickey puts the cruel side of nature and the cruel side of men together in his stories and poems to shock his readers.

CULTURAL NOTES

Perhaps the world's most famous tree house is the one that Tarzan built. Tarzan of the Apes was an imaginary character created by a writer named Edgar Rice Burroughs. Tarzan was a human being whose parents died. He grew up in the African jungle, and he learned how to survive in the animal world. He built and lived in a wonderful tree house.

A tree house requires a special kind of tree: one with a long trunk and spreading branches. Wooden steps are nailed to the trunk. A floor is built on the spreading branches. Sometimes walls and a roof are added. But most tree houses are simply wooden floors, held up by the branches of the tree.

Very few people live in tree houses all the time. Most people — especially young boys — use them for escape: to leave the earth for awhile, and to live above the ground with birds and the sounds of the wind.

STRATEGIES

"In the Tree House at Night" is a poem about three brothers. One brother, the poet, has built a tree house. The second brother is asleep in the tree house. The third brother is dead. His spirit and memory made the poet build the tree house. The dead brother has become the spirit of the tree and of the tree house, which is a memorial to him. Here are some questions to guide you as read the poem:

What time is it?

Who is physically present? Who is physically absent?

Who has built the tree house?

Did the dead brother die before or after the tree house was built?

What did the dead brother tell the two living brothers?

How does the poet (I) compare the dead brother and the pine tree?

Which lines present the ideas of sleep? Of something strange or unusual? Of the puzzle of life and death?

In the last stanza, the poet asks three questions. Do any of them have answers within the poem itself?

How can someone be alone and with others at the same time?

The last line of the poem uses the image "The heart of the world." What do you think the poet means?

In the Tree House at Night

James Dickey

1 And now the green household is dark.
2 The half-moon completely is shining
3 On the earth-lighted tops of the trees.
4 To be dead, a house must be still.
5 The floor and the walls wave me slowly;
6 I am deep in them over my head.
7 The needles and pine cones about me

8 Are full of small birds at their roundest,
9 Their *fists* without *mercy* gripping
10 Hard down through the tree to the roots
11 To sing back at light when they feel it.
12 We lie here like angels in bodies,
13 My brothers and I, one dead,
14 The other asleep from much living,

15 In mid-air *huddled* beside me.
16 Dark climbed to us here as we climbed
17 Up the nails I have hammered all day
18 Through the *sprained, comic rungs* of the ladder
19 Of *broom handles, crate slats, and laths*
20 Foot by foot up the trunk to the branches
21 Where we came out at last over lakes

fists — claws
mercy — kindness
huddled — curled up
sprained, comic rungs — twisted, funny-looking steps
broom handles, crate slats, and laths — odd pieces of wood

22   Of leaves, of fields *disencumbered of earth*
23   That move with the *moves of the spirit*.
24   Each nail that *sustains* us I set here;
25   Each nail in the house is now *steadied*
26   By my dead brother's huge, *freckled* hand.
27   Through the years, he has pointed his hammer
28   Up into these limbs, and told us

29   That we must *ascend*, and all lie here.
30   Step after step he has brought me,
31   *Embracing* the trunk as his body,
32   Shaking its limbs with my heartbeat,
33   Till the pine cones danced without wind
34   And fell from the branches like apples.
35   In the *arm-slender forks* of our dwelling

36   I breathe my live brother's *light hair*.
37   The blanket around us becomes
38   As solid as stone, and it *sways*,
39   With all my heart, I close
40   The blue, timeless *eye of my mind*.
41   Wind *springs*, as my dead brother smiles
42   And touches the tree at the root;

---

disencumbered of earth — separated from earth
moves of the spirit — the spirit of life
sustains — holds, supports
steadied — kept steady or secure
freckled — spotted with freckles (brown spots)
ascend — climb up
embracing — holding closely
arm-slender forks — branches like thin arms
light hair — light-colored (blond)
sways — moves slowly
eye of my mind — "mind's eye"; memory
springs — rises quickly

43 A *shudder of joy* runs up
44 The trunk; the needles *tingle*;
45 One bird *uncontrollably cries.*
46 The *wind changes round*, and I stir
47 Within another's life. Whose life?
48 Who is dead? Whose *presence* is living?
49 *When may I fall strangely* to earth,

50 Who am nailed to this branch by a spirit?
51 Can two bodies make up a third?
52 *To sing, must I feel the world's light?*
53 My green, graceful bones fill the air
54 With sleeping birds. Alone, alone
55 And with them I move gently.
56 I move at the heart of the world.

RETELLING

James Dickey's poem "_____ _____

_____ _____ _____

_____" is about three _____. Two are

_____ and one is _____. The

_____ brother believed that they should

_____ a _____ _____.

---

shudder of joy—trembling of pleasure
tingle—shake
uncontrollably cries—sings without being able to stop
wind changes round—literally, changes its direction; figuratively, takes me somewhere else.
presence—something (as a spirit) felt to be present
when may I fall strangely—figuratively, when may I become myself?
To sing, must I feel the world's light?—Must I sing (poetry) at dawn, in daylight? May I sing in darkness, too?

However, the _____ brother did not

_____ it. The _____ built it. He

_____ steps on the tree _____. He and

his _____ brother _____ together in the

_____ _____. But the

_____ brother is also _____. He is a

_____. He is _____ missing. He lives in

the _____ and the _____ of the

_____. The poet asks who is _____ and

whose _____ is _____. Can two

_____ make up a _____? The poet tells

us that a house must be _____ to be

_____. But this house _____, and it is

filled with _____. So in the end, we may

_____, "Who *really* _____ the

_____ _____?" "Is _____

stronger than _____?"

STRUCTURE AND STYLE

Connections

1. Each stanza of James Dickey's poem has seven lines. What happens in the seventh line of every stanza *except* the seventh line of stanza 6? If you *stop* at the end of line seven in the other stanzas, what happens to the meaning of those lines?

2. "In the Tree House at Night" depends on several *contrasts* — things or persons that show differences when we look at them. In the left column below, there are words from the poem which contrast with other words in the poem. Write those other words in the right column.

   a. dark   _____

   b. earth   _____

   c. still   _____

   d. dead   _____

   e. bodies   _____

   f. asleep (sleeping)   _____

   g. climb/ascend   _____

   h. root/trunk   _____

   i. alone   _____

3. The poem also depends on *comparisons* — things or persons that show similarities when we look at them. Sometimes these similarities are presented as *similes* and *metaphors* — "figurative" uses of language. Find the similarities between the words and phrases given (left column) and others in the poem. Write the others in the right column.

   a. birds sing   _____

   b. human bodies   _____

   c. foot by foot (measurement) _____

   d. tree limbs   _____

   e. tree trunk   _____

   f. tree leaves   _____

   g. we climbed   _____

   h. movement (physical)   _____

   i. the poet's (my) hand   _____

j. nailed (pieces of wood)   _____

k. heart (human)   _____

LAST WORDS

The poet asks himself some difficult questions about life and death. We come to realize that the poet lives with his brother's spirit. This spirit, this presence, is very powerful: "(I) am nailed to this branch by a spirit."

Do you feel that there is a *communion* (a sense of harmony, a feeling of friendship) at the end of the poem? Which lines give you this feeling?

II
WORK

6

THE PARSLEY GARDEN

William Saroyan

William Saroyan

HEAD NOTES

One of the most productive writers in American literary history, William Saroyan (1908–1981) wrote over four hundred short stores as well as plays and novels. For a period of time he wrote a story a day, and he did not revise his work. He began writing when he was thirteen years old, left high school at fifteen, and never went to college. He wrote about his own family and other people he knew in Fresno, a small city in the middle of California's farming region. Many Armenians immigrated to Fresno from Europe, including the Saroyan family, and Saroyan often wrote about the difficulties of being a foreigner in the United States. He said that his stories were allegories. They were stories about specific people, but they suggested something about the human condition—the lives of all people. Saroyan was awarded the Pulitzer Prize for his play, *The Time of Your Life*, but he refused it, saying he didn't believe that his art should be paid for by rich people. One of Saroyan's most popular novels, *The Human Comedy*, was made into a movie.

CULTURAL NOTES

This story, like most of Saroyan's stories, takes place in California in the town of Fresno. Farming and shipping fruits and vegetables were the most important businesses in and around Fresno fifty years ago. Saroyan is writing about the lives of a boy and his mother during the Depression years—the 1930s in America. Mrs. Condraj, Al's mother, depends on work at Foley's Packing House, where fruit is put in crates and boxes for shipment by train to the East Coast. She works a long day for only a few dollars. Al Condraj, her son, is only eleven years old, and he has no job. He walks around town; it is summer and school is out; Al has very little to do. He wants to do something for his mother. In Woolworth's department store, a big store that sells things for low prices, Al steals a hammer. He knows that he is stealing it. He doesn't have ten cents to pay for it. And Al gets caught. Saroyan lets us share Al's feelings as Al and his mother work out his problem.

STRATEGIES

William Saroyan tells "The Parsley Garden" from Al's *point-of-view*. That is, Saroyan shows us Al's experiences as Al has them. Saroyan puts us inside Al so that we can share his feelings.

There is an important difference between a story told by "I" and a story told by "He." A *first-person* ("I") story has its limits. Everything that happens is the experience of the story-teller. Any actions or thoughts that "I" can't experience cannot be written. A *third-person* ("He") story has fewer limitations. The story-teller is not the person having the experiences. "He" is having the experiences, and the story-teller can make him and all other characters do and think whatever is necessary for the story's development. Thus, the story-teller has more freedom to invent.

Saroyan has created a young boy, Al Condraj, who lives with his mother in a small town. Their house is small, too—only three rooms. They have very little money. Al's mother speaks "broken English"; that is, she makes mistakes when she speaks. She says "Shut up" whenever she doesn't know what else to say.

As you read "The Parsley Garden" let these questions guide your reading:

What has Al Condraj collected from Foley's Packing House?

Why does he think he needs a hammer?

How does Al take the hammer from Woolworth's?

How is Al caught?

How is Al treated by the younger man?

How is Al treated by the older man?

How does Al feel?

Why does he plan to return to the store?

Why does he give up this plan?

When Al gets home, why doesn't he go inside?

What is the parsley garden?

When Al tells his mother what he has done, what does she tell him?

How does Al feel?

What does Al's mother think about his experiences?

How does Al get the hammer?

How does he feel about this experience?

Why do think this story is called "The Parsley Garden?"

it's center of their world or life

The Parsley Garden

William Saroyan

---

1   One day in August Al Condraj was *wandering* through *Woolworth's* without a penny to spend when he saw a small hammer that was not a toy but a real hammer and he was *possessed with a longing* to have it. He believed it was just what he needed by which to break the *monotony* and with which to make something. He had gathered some first-class nails from *Foley's Packing House* where the boxmakers worked and where they had carelessly dropped at least fifteen cents' worth. He had gladly *gone to the trouble* of gathering them together because it had seemed to him that a nail, as such, was not something to be *wasted*. He had the nails, perhaps a half pound of them, at least two hundred of them, in a paper bag in the apple box in which he kept his *junk* at home.

2   Now, with the ten-cent hammer he believed he could make something out of box wood and the nails, although he had no idea what. Some sort of a table perhaps, or a small bench.

3   At any rate he took the hammer and slipped it into the pocket of his *overalls*, but just as he did so a man took him firmly by the arm without a word and pushed him to the back of the store into a small office. Another man, an older one, was seated behind a desk in the office, working with papers. The younger man, the one who had *captured* him, was excited and his forehead was covered with sweat.

4   "Well," he said, *"here's one more of them."*

5   The man behind the desk got to his feet and looked Al Condraj up and down.

---

wandering — walking without any place to go
Woolworth's — a large department store
possessed with a longing — felt a strong desire
monotony — boredom
Foley's Packing House — a place that shipped fruits and vegetables
gone to the trouble — made an effort
wasted — thrown away
junk — things of little value
overalls — work clothes
captured — caught
here's one more of them — here's another thief

6   "What's he *swiped*?"

7   "A hammer." The young man looked at Al with hatred. "Hand it over," he said.

8   The boy brought the hammer out of his pocket and handed it to the young man, who said, "I ought to hit you over the head with it, that's what I ought to do."

9   He turned to the older man, the boss, the manager of the store, and he said, "What do you want me to do with him?"

10   "Leave him with me," the older man said.

11   The younger man stepped out of the office, and the older man sat down and went back to work. Al Condraj stood in the office fifteen minutes before the older man looked at him again.

12   "Well," he said.

13   Al didn't know what to say. The man wasn't looking at him, he was looking at the door.

14   Finally Al said, "I didn't mean to steal it. I just need it and I haven't got any money."

15   "Just because you haven't got money doesn't mean *you've got a right* to steal things," the man said. "Now, does it?"

16   "No, sir."

17   "Well, what am I going to do with you? *Turn you over* to the police?"

18   Al didn't say anything, but he certainly didn't want to be turned over to the police. He hated the man, but at the same time he realized somebody else could be a lot *tougher* than he was being.

19   "If I let you go, will you promise never to steal from this store again?"

20   "Yes, sir."

21   "All right," The man said. "Go out this way and don't come back to this store until you've got some money to spend."

---

swiped — stolen (slang)
you've got a right — you have permission
turn you over — give you
tougher — meaner; more difficult

22 He opened a door to the hall that led to the *alley*, and Al Condraj hurried down the hall and out into the alley.

23 The first thing he did when he was free was laugh, but he knew he had been *humiliated* and he was deeply ashamed. It was not in his nature to take things that did not belong to him. He hated the young man who had caught him and he hated the manager of the store who had made him stand in silence in the office so long. He hadn't liked it at all when the young man had said he ought to hit him over the head with the hammer.

24 He should have had the *courage* to look him straight in the eye and say, *"You and who else?"*

25 Of course he <u>had</u> stolen the hammer and he had been caught, but it seemed to him he oughtn't to have been so humiliated.

26 After he had walked three blocks he decided he didn't want to go home *just yet*, so he turned around and started walking back to town. He almost believed he meant to go back and say something to the young man who had caught him. And then he wasn't sure he didn't mean to go back and steal the hammer again, and this time <u>not</u> get caught. As long as he had been made to feel like a thief anyway, *the least* he ought to get out of it was the hammer.

27 Outside the store he *lost his nerve*, though. He stood in the street, looking in, for at least ten minutes.

28 Then, *crushed and confused* and now *bitterly* ashamed of himself, first for having stolen something, then for having been caught, then for having been humiliated, then for *not having guts enough* to go back and *do the job right*, he began walking home again, his mind so *troubled* that he didn't greet his pal Pete Wawchek when they *came face to face* outside Graf's Hardware.

---

alley—narrow street
humiliated—made to feel low and bad
courage—inner strength
You and who else?—you aren't strong enough to do it yourself
just yet—at that time
the least—the smallest thing
lost his nerve—became afraid
crushed and confused—powerless and uncertain
bitterly—harshly, intensely
not having guts enough—lacking courage (slang)
do the job right—succeed
troubled—upset
came face to face—met each other

29   When he got home he was too ashamed to go inside and examine his junk, so he had a long drink of water from the *faucet* in the back yard. The faucet was used by his mother to water the *stuff* she planted every year: okra, bell peppers, tomatoes, cucumbers, onions, garlic, mint, eggplants, and parsley.

30   His mother called *the whole business* the parsley garden, and every night in the summer she would bring chairs out of the house and put them around the table she had had Ondro, the neighborhood *handyman,* make for her for fifteen cents, and she would sit at the table and enjoy the cool of the garden and the smell of the things she had planted and *tended*.

31   Sometimes she would even make a salad and moisten the flat *old-country bread* and slice some white cheese, and she and he would have supper in the parsley garden. After supper she would attach the water hose to the faucet and water her plants and the place would be cooler than *ever* and it would smell real good, real fresh and cool and green, all the different growing things making a green-garden smell out of themselves and the air and the water.

32   After the long drink of water he sat down where the parsley itself was growing and he pulled a handful of it out and slowly ate it. Then he went inside and told his mother what had happened. He even told her what he had <u>thought</u> of doing after he had been turned loose: to go back and steal the hammer again.

33   "I don't want you to steal," his mother said in broken English. "Here is ten cents. You go back to that man and you give him this money and you bring it home, that hammer."

34   "No," Al Condraj said. "I won't take your money for something I don't really need. I just thought I ought to have a hammer, so I could make something *if I felt like it*. I've got a lot of nails and some box wood, but I haven't got a hammer."

35   "Go buy it, that hammer," his mother said.

---

faucet — iron pipe for carrying water
stuff — things
the whole business — everything; all the plants
handyman — someone who does all kinds of work
tended — looked after
old-country bread — Armenian bread, in this case
ever — before
if I felt like it — if I wanted to

36   "No," Al said.

37   "All right," his mother said. *"Shut up."*

38   That's what she always said when she didn't know what else to say.

39   Al went out and sat on the steps. His humiliation was beginning to really hurt now. He decided to wander off along the railroad tracks to Foley's because he needed to think about it some more. At Foley's he watched Johnny Gale nailing boxes for ten minutes, but Johnny was too busy to notice him or talk to him, although one day at Sunday school, two or three years ago, Johnny had greeted him and said, "How's the boy?" Johnny worked with a boxmaker's *hatchet* and everybody in Fresno said he was the fastest boxmaker in town. He was the *closest thing to a machine* any packing house ever saw. Foley himself was proud of Johnny Gale.

40   Al Condraj finally set out for home because he didn't want to *get in the way*. He didn't want somebody working hard to notice that he was being watched and maybe say to him, "Go on, *beat it*." He didn't want Johnny Gale to do something like that. He didn't want to invite another humiliation.

41   On the way home he looked for money but all he found was the usual pieces of broken glass and rusty nails, the things that were always cutting his bare feet every summer.

42   When he got home his mother had made a salad and set the table, so he sat down to eat, but when he put the food in his mouth he just *didn't care for it*. He got up and went into the three-room house and got his apple box out of the corner of his room and went through his junk. It was all there, the same as yesterday.

43   He wandered off back to town and stood in front of the closed store, hating the young man who had caught him, and then he went along to the *Hippodrome* and looked at the display photographs from the two movies that were being shown that day.

---

shut up—keep your mouth closed; be quiet
hatchet—a small axe
closest thing to a machine—very much like a machine
get in the way—be a nuisance; cause a problem
beat it—go away (slang)
didn't care for it—lost his appetite
Hippodrome—a movie theater

44   Then he went along to the public library to have a look at all the books again, but he didn't like any of them, so he wandered around town *some more*, and then around half-past eight he went home and went to bed.

45   His mother had already gone to bed because she had to be up at five to go to work at *Inderrieden's*, packing *figs*. Some days there would be work all day, some days there would be only half a day of it, but whatever his mother *earned* during the summer had to *keep them* the whole year.

46   He didn't sleep much that night because he couldn't get over what had happened, and he went over six or seven ways by which to adjust the matter. He *went so far as to believe* it would be necessary to kill the young man who had caught him. He also believed it would be necessary for him to steal *systematically* and successfully the rest of his life. It was a hot night and he couldn't sleep.

47   Finally, his mother got up and walked *barefooted* to the kitchen for a drink of water and on the way back she said to him softly, "Shut up."

48   When she got up at five in the morning he was *out of the house*, but that had happened many times before. He was a *restless* boy, and he kept moving all the time every summer. He was making mistakes and *paying for them*, and he had just tried stealing and had been caught at it and he was troubled. She fixed her breakfast, packed her lunch and hurried off to work, hoping it would be a *full day*.

49   It was a full day, and then there was *overtime*, and although she had no more lunch she decided to *work on* for the extra money, anyway. Almost all the packers were staying on, too, and her neighbor across the alley, Leeza Ahboot, who worked beside her, said, "Let us work until the work stops, then we'll go home and fix a supper between us and eat it in your

---

some more—for more time
Inderrieden's—a packing house
figs—a kind of fruit that grows in hot dry climates
earned—made (money)
keep them—pay their living costs
went so far as to believe—imagined
systematically—routinely; as a way of life
barefooted—without shoes
out of the house—had gone
restless—active
paying for them—suffering as a result
full day—eight hours
overtime—more than eight hours and extra pay
work on—continue to work

parsley garden where it's so cool. It's a hot day and there's *no sense not making* an extra fifty or sixty cents."

50   When the two women reached the garden it was almost nine o'clock, but still daylight, and she saw her son nailing pieces of box wood together, making something with a hammer. It looked like a bench. He had already watered the garden and *tidied up* the rest of the yard, and the place seemed very nice, and her son seemed very serious and busy. She and Leeza went *straight to work for their supper*, picking bell peppers and tomatoes and cucumbers and a great deal of parsley for the salad.

51   Then Leeza went to her house for some bread which she had baked the night before, and some white cheese, and in a few minutes they were having supper together and talking pleasantly about the successful day they had had. After supper, they made Turkish coffee over an open fire in the yard. They drank the coffee and smoked a *cigarette apiece*, and told one another stories about their experiences in the old country and here in Fresno, and then they looked into their cups at the *grounds* to see if any good fortune was *indicated*, and there was: health and work and supper out of doors in the summer and enough money for the rest of the year.

52   Al Condraj worked and *overheard* some of the things they said, and then Leeza went home to go to bed, and his mother said, "Where you get it, that hammer, Al?"

53   "I got it at the store."

54   "How you get it? You steal it?"

55   Al Condraj finished the bench and sat on it. "No," he said. "I didn't steal it."

56   "How you get it?"

57   "I worked at the store for it," Al said.

58   "The store where you steal it yesterday?"

59   "Yes."

---

no sense not making — it is sensible to continue working
tidied up — cleaned
straight to work for their supper — started making supper immediately
cigarette apiece — one cigarette each
grounds — bits of coffee beans
indicated — shown
overheard — heard without their knowing

60   "Who give you job?"

61   "The boss."

62   "What you do?"

63   "I carried different stuff to the different *counters*."

64   "Well, that's good," the woman said. "How long you work for that little hammer?"

65   "I worked all day," Al said. "Mr. Clemmer gave me the hammer after I'd worked one hour, but I went right on working. The fellow who caught me yesterday showed me what to do, and we worked together. We didn't talk, but at the end of the day he took me to Mr. Clemmer's office and he told Mr. Clemmer that I'd worked hard all day and ought to be paid at least a dollar."

66   "That's good," the woman said.

67   "So Mr. Clemmer put a silver dollar on his desk for me, and then the fellow who caught me yesterday told him the store needed a boy like me every day, for a dollar a day, and Mr. Clemmer said I could have the job."

68   "That's good," the woman said. "You can make it a little money for yourself."

69   "I left the dollar on Mr. Clemmer's desk," Al Condraj said, "and I told them both I didn't want the job."

70   "Why you say that?" the woman said. "Dollar a day for eleven-year-old-boy good money. Why you not take job?"

71   "Because I hate the both of them," the boy said. "I would never work for people like that. I just looked at them and picked up my hammer and walked out. I came home and I made this bench."

72   "All right," his mother said. "Shut up."

73   His mother went inside and went to bed, but Al Condraj sat on the bench he had made and smelled the parsley garden and didn't feel humiliated any more.

---

counters—places where things are sold

74 But nothing could stop him from hating the two men, even though he knew they hadn't done anything *they shouldn't have done.*

RETELLING

Al Condraj _____ things and put them in an

_____ _____. This is where he kept his

_____. Al has _____ some

_____ from _____ _____

_____. He needed a _____ so that he

could _____ something.

He _____ the _____ he

_____ at Woolworth's. He put it into the

_____ of his _____. He _____

the _____, and he got _____.

Al told the store _____ that he didn't

_____ to steal the _____. He

_____ have _____ _____.

That was not a good _____.

The _____ manager let Al _____

because Al _____ never to _____ from

that store _____.

Al felt _____ and _____. He

_____ both of the men at Woolworth's. He

---

they shouldn't have done—they did what was right

_____ to return to the _____ and

_____ the hammer again. This time he wouldn't

_____ _____. But he couldn't

_____ the store, and finally he _____

_____. He felt _____ and

_____.

When he got _____ he sat for awhile in the

_____ _____. Then he _____

his _____ what had _____ at the

_____. His mother offered him _____

_____ so that he could _____ the

_____. But he _____.

During the next day, while his _____ was

_____ at a fruit _____ house, Al

_____ to Woolworth's. He _____ all day,

and he _____ a _____. The

_____ offered him a job, but Al didn't

_____ his offer. Al also _____ the

_____ they offered him. Instead, Al _____

the _____ and went home.

Al's mother was _____ with Al's work, but she

wondered why he didn't _____ the

_____. Al told her that he _____ both of

the _____ at Woolworth's. He came

_____ and made a _____. Al didn't feel

_____ any more, but he still _____ the

_____ _____.

STRUCTURE AND STYLE

Connections: Modals

1. Saroyan's story about Al's experience uses the words *should*, *would*, and *ought to* with verbs. These words change the meanings of verbs and sentences. Study this pair of sentences.

   a. He *went* to the store.

   b. He *should have gone* to the store.

   Sentence (a) is a report of an action, a fact. Sentence (b) says something else: he meant to go; he had an obligation to go; but he *didn't* go. The action did not happen.

   The modal *would* contrasts with *would have*. Study this pair of sentences.

   c. She *would* make a salad.

   d. She *would have* made a salad.

   Sentence (c) is a report of an action that is a custom, a habit. It is an action that is repeated often. Sentence (d) says something else. Something kept her from making a salad: perhaps she came home late, or there was nothing to eat. She *didn't* make a salad. The action did not happen.

   The modal *ought to* is similar to *should* (have). Study this pair of sentences.

   e. I *will* leave in five minutes.

   f. I *ought to* leave in five minutes.

   Sentence (e) states a purpose. It is definite. Sentence (f) states an obligation. It is not definite: I *ought to* leave. Maybe I will, or maybe I will not.

2. Now look at these sentences from "The Parsley Garden." Answer this question: Did the action happen or didn't it happen?

   a. I ought to hit you over the head with it.

   b. He should·have had the courage to look him straight in the eye.

   c. He oughtn't to have been so humiliated.

    d. The least he ought to get out of it is the hammer.

    e. She would bring chairs out of the house.

    f. She and he would have supper in the parsley garden.

    g. I just thought I ought to have a hammer.

    h. Some days there would be work all day.

    i. I would never work for people like that.

    j. They hadn't done anything they shouldn't have done.

Now rewrite all the preceding sentences in which the action didn't happen. Rewrite them as definite reports of an action that did happen or will happen.

LAST WORDS

Saroyan says, "Of course he had stolen the hammer and he had been caught, but it seemed to him he oughtn't to have been so humiliated."

Why is humiliation worse than stealing and being caught in Al's mind?

Saroyan tells us what Al's mother thinks about Al: "He was making mistakes and paying for them, and he had just tried stealing and had been caught at it and he was troubled."

How does Al's mother feel about what Al has done? At the end of the story, "(Al) . . . didn't feel humiliated any more. But nothing could stop him from hating the two men . . .".

Why does Al continue to hate the two men? He knows that they did what they had to do. And he has worked all day to earn the hammer. Why isn't the problem solved?

7

THE DEATH OF THE HIRED MAN

Robert Frost

Robert Frost

HEAD NOTES

The American poet Robert Frost (1874–1963) received a gold medal from the U.S. Senate in 1950 because "his poems have helped to guide American thought and humor and wisdom . . .". He was invited to read his poetry at the Presidential Inauguration of John F. Kennedy in 1961. No poet had ever been part of this ceremony before. Frost won two Pulitzer Prizes for Poetry and many other prizes as well, beginning in high school when he was chosen top student and was asked to give the graduation speech. His poems use the common language that people speak, and he wrote about everyday people doing everyday activities. He was a regionalist, writing about the people of New England, the region he knew best. He never dealt with politics or religion in his poems. He said that he began his poems with a feeling and he made the feeling into words. His poetry is rich in metaphor, a way of using words to say something greater and different than the words themselves appear to mean at first. For example, in one of his famous poems, "The Road Not Taken," he writes about two roads in a forest to speak about choices we make in our lives.

CULTURAL NOTES

This is a narrative poem—a poem that tells a story. The setting is a New England farm, perhaps in Vermont or New Hampshire. Farming in New England is difficult. The fields are rocky, and the weather is uncertain. Many New England farms are small; they are "family farms." The farmers make a living, but they rarely make much money.

During harvest season—usually late summer or early fall—farmers may hire a man or two to help with the harvest. A hired man may live with the farm family for several weeks. He is paid wages; and he has a place to live—a bunkhouse or a spare room.

The farm in this poem produces hay: grass that is cut and dried as food for animals. In the early part of the twentieth century, haying was done mostly by men and farm animals. Farm machines like tractors came later. It is this early period of time that Frost is describing in "The Death of the Hired Man."

STRATEGIES

Frost's poem is several poems in one. It is a study of three characters: Warren, the farmer; his wife, Mary; and Silas, the hired man. It is a conversation between Warren and Mary. And it is a little one-act play. The reader is listening to an argument between Warren and Mary. They are arguing about Silas. He never appears, and yet we learn a great deal about him.

As you read this poem, you must understand the argument between Warren and Mary. It is a dialogue. You must understand which character—Warren or Mary—is speaking. Sometimes the poet—the narrator—speaks, too. It will help you to label the parts of the dialogue *W, M,* or *N.*

Here are some questions to guide your reading of the poem:

Warren does not want to hire Silas again. What are his reasons (lines 12–24)?

Mary wants to help Silas. What are her reasons (lines 33–39; 114–115; 154–160; 163–166)?

At an earlier time, Silas had a conflict with a boy named Harold Wilson, another "hired man." What were the reasons for this conflict (lines 61–90; 99–101)?

Silas has a rich brother. Why doesn't Silas ask his brother for help (lines 133–152)?

How did you expect the argument to end? How does the argument end (line 175)?

The Death of the Hired Man

Robert Frost

1   Mary sat *musing on* the lamp-flame at the table
2   Waiting for Warren. When she heard his step,
3   She ran *on tip-toe* down the darkened passage
4   To meet him in the doorway with the news
5   And *put him on his guard.* "Silas *is back.*"
6   She pushed him outward with her through the door
7   And shut it after her. "Be kind," she said.
8   She took the *market things* from Warren's arms
9   And set them on the porch, then drew him down
10 To sit beside her on the wooden steps.
11 "When was I ever anything but kind to him?
- 12 But I'll not have the fellow back," he said.
13 "I told him so *last haying*, didn't I?
14 'If he left then,' I said, 'that ended it.'
15 (What good is he? Who else will *harbor* him
16 At his age for the little he can do?
17 What help he is there's no depending on.
18 Off he goes always when I need him most.
19 'He thinks he ought to earn a little pay,
20 Enough at least to buy tobacco with,
21 So he won't have to beg and be *beholden.*'
22 "All right,' I say, 'I can't afford to pay
23 Any *fixed wages*, though I wish I could.'
- 24 'Someone else can.' 'Then someone else will have to.'

---

musing on — thinking about
on tip-toe — quickly and quietly
put him on his guard — warned him
is back — has returned
market things — purchases from the store
last haying — last year when grass was cut for hay
harbor — give (him) a place to stay
beholden — in debt to someone
fixed wages — regular payments of a certain amount

25   I shouldn't mind his *bettering* himself
26   *If that was what it was*. You can be certain,
27   When he begins like that, there's someone *at him*
28   Trying to *coax him off with pocket-money*,—
29   In haying time, when any help is scarce.
30   In winter he comes back to us. I'm *done*."

31   "Sh! not so loud: he'll hear you," Mary said.

32   "I want him to: he'll have to *soon or late*."

33   "He's worn out. He's asleep beside the stove.
34   When I came up from Rowe's I found him here,
35   *Huddled* against the barn-door fast asleep,
36   A *miserable* sight, and frightening, too—
37   You needn't smile—I didn't recognize him—
38   I wasn't looking for him—and he's changed.
39   Wait till you see."

40   "Where did you say he'd been?"

41   "He didn't say. I dragged him to the house,
42   And gave him tea and tried to make him smoke.
43   I tried to make him talk about his travels,
44   Nothing would *do*: he just kept *nodding off*."

45   "What did he say? Did he say anything?"

46   "*But little*."

---

bettering—improving
if that was what it was—if it was improvement
at him—after him; pursuing him
coax him off with pocket money—buy his labor for a little extra money
done—finished with him
soon or late—sooner or later; at some time
huddled—curled up
miserable—very sad
do—succeed
nodding off—going to sleep
But little—only a little

47   "Anything? Mary, *confess*
48 He said he'd come to *ditch the meadow* for me."

49 "Warren!"

50   "But did he? I just want to know."

51 "Of course he did. What would you *have him say*?
52 Surely you wouldn't *grudge* the poor old man
53 Some *humble* way to save his self-respect.
54 He added, if you really care to know,
55 He meant to *clear the upper pasture*, too.
56 That sounds like something you have heard before?
57 Warren, I wish you could have heard the way
58 He *jumbled* everything. I stopped to look
59 Two or three times—he made me feel so *queer*—
60 To see if he was talking in his sleep.

61 He *ran on* Harold Wilson—you remember—
62 The boy you had in haying four years *since*.
63 He's finished school, and teaching in his college.
64 Silas declares you'll have to get *him* back.
65 He says they two will make a team for work:
66 Between them they will *lay this farm as smooth*!
67 The way he mixed that in with other things.

---

confess—tell the truth
ditch the meadow—dig a ditch in grassy land (to drain it)
have him say—want him to say
grudge—stop (him) from having
humble—ordinary; simple
clear the upper pasture—clean the place where cows eat grass
jumbled—mixed up
queer—strange; unusual
ran on—talked about
since—ago
him—Harold Wilson
lay this farm as smooth—make the farm successful

68   He thinks young Wilson a likely lad, though *daft*
69   *On education*—you know how they fought
70   All through July under the blazing sun,
71   Silas up on the cart to *build* the load,
72   Harold along beside to *pitch* it on."

73   "Yes, I took care to keep *well out of earshot*."

74   "Well, those days trouble Silas like a dream.
75   You wouldn't think they would. How some things *linger*!
76   Harold's young college boy's *assurance piqued* him.
77   After so many years he still keeps finding
78   Good arguments he sees he might have used.
79   I sympathize. I know just how it feels
80   To think of the right thing to say too late.
81   Harold's *associated* in his mind with Latin.
82   He asked me what I thought of Harold's saying
83   He studied Latin like the violin
84   Because he liked it—*that an argument*!
85   He said he couldn't make the boy believe
86   He could find water with a *hazel prong*—
87   Which showed how much good school had ever done him.
88   He wanted to go over that. But most of all
89   He thinks if he could have another chance
90   To teach him how to build a load of hay—"

---

daft on education—made crazy by book-learning
build—stack; put in place
pitch—throw (with a pitchfork)
well out of earshot—unable to be heard
linger—stay; remain
assurance—self-confidence
piqued—bothered; upset
associated—mixed
that an argument—here, what a silly idea
hazel prong—a forked stick of (hazel) wood used to locate water under
   the ground

91   "I know, that's Silas' one *accomplishment*.

92   He bundles every forkful in its place,

93   And *tags and numbers it for future reference*,

94   So he can find and easily *dislodge* it

95   In the unloading. Silas does that well.

96   He takes it out in bunches like birds' nests.

97   You never see him standing on the hay

98   He's trying to lift, *straining* to lift himself."

99   "*He* thinks if he could teach *him* that, he'd be

100   Some good perhaps to someone in the world.

101   He hates to see a boy the *fool of books*.

102   Poor Silas, so concerned for other folk,

103   And nothing to look backward to with pride,

104   And nothing to look forward to with hope,

105   *So now and never any different*."

106   Part of a moon was falling down the west,

107   Dragging the whole sky with it to the hills.

108   Its light poured softly in her lap. She saw

109   And spread her apron to it. She put out her hand   —

110   Among the harp-like *morning-glory strings*,

111   Taut with the dew from garden bed to *eaves*,

112   As if she played unheard some tenderness

113   That *wrought* on him beside her in the night.   —

114   "Warren," she said, "he has come home to die:

115   You needn't be afraid he'll leave you this time."

---

accomplishment—skill or ability
tags and numbers it for future reference—remembers where he put it
dislodge—here, take it out
straining—trying very hard
He—Silas
him—Harold Wilson
fool of books—not practical
so now and never any different—this way now and always
lines 109–113—Frost uses the metaphor of a harp made of vines that Mary
    plays
morning-glory strings—the stems of a vine with large blue flowers
eaves—the edges of the roof
wrought—worked

116   "Home," he *mocked* gently.

117   "Yes, what else but home?
118   It all depends on what you mean by home.
119   Of course he's nothing to us, any more
120   Than was the hound that came a stranger to us
121   Out of the woods, worn out upon the trail."

122   "Home is the place where, when you have to go there,
123   They have to take you in."

124   "I should have called it
125   Something you somehow haven't to deserve."

126   Warren leaned out and took a step or two,
127   Picked up a little stick, and brought it back
128   And broke it in his hand and tossed it *by.*
129   "Silas has *better claim on us*, you think,
130   Than on his brother? Thirteen little miles
131   As the road winds would bring him to *his* door.
132   Silas has walked that far no doubt today.
133   Why didn't he go there? His brother's rich,
134   *A somebody*—director in the bank."

135   "He never told us that."

136   "We know it though."

137   "I think his brother ought to help, of course.

---

mocked—made fun of (Mary)
by—nearby
better claim on us—more reason to come to us
his—his brother's
a somebody—an important person

138 I'll see to that if there is need. He *ought of right*
139 To take *him* in, and might be willing to—
140 He may be *better than appearances*.
141 But have some pity on Silas. Do you think
142 If he'd had any pride in *claiming kin*
143 Or anything he *looked for* from his brother,
144 He'd keep so *still* about him all this time?"

145 "I wonder *what's between them*."

146   "I can tell you
147 Silas is what he is—we wouldn't *mind him*—
148 But just the kind that kinsfolk can't *abide*.
149 He never did a thing so very bad.
150 He *don't* know why he isn't quite as good
151 As anyone. Worthless though he is,
152 He won't be made ashamed to please his brother."

153 "I can't think Si ever hurt anyone."

154 "No, but he hurt my heart the way he lay
155 And rolled his old head on that sharp-edged chair-back.
156 He wouldn't let me put him on the *lounge*.
157 You must go in and see what you can do.
158 I made the bed up for him there tonight.
159 You'll be surprised at him—how much he's *broken*.
160 His working days are *done*; I'm sure of it."

---

ought of right—should surely
him—Silas
better than appearances—a better person than he seems to be
claiming kin—asking a relative for help
looked for—expected
still—quiet
what's between them—what kind of relationship they have
mind him—object to him; dislike him
abide—accept
don't—doesn't
lounge—sofa
broken—sick and tired
done—finished; over

161   "I'd not be in a hurry to say that."

162   "I haven't been. Go, look, see for yourself.
163   But, Warren, please remember how it is:
164   He's come to help you ditch the meadow.
165   He has a plan. You mustn't laugh at him.
166   He may not speak of it, and then he may.
167   I'll sit and see if that small sailing cloud
168   Will hit or miss the moon."

169   It hit the moon.
170   Then there were three there, making a dim row,
171   The moon, the little silver cloud, and she.

172   Warren returned—too soon, it seemed to her,
173   *Slipped* to her side, *caught up* her hand and waited.

174   "Warren?" she questioned.

175   "Dead," was all he answered.

RETELLING

_____, the farmer, and _____, his

wife, have an __argument__ about Silas, the

__hired_____ __man_____. Mary _____

Silas, and she wants him to _____. Warren will not

_____ Silas again, because Silas is _____;

and Silas _____ when he is needed. Silas returns in

---

slipped—moved quickly
caught up—grasped and held tightly

_____. Warren says, "I'm done." He means

_____ _____.

Mary has _____ for Silas because he is

_____. She tells Warren that Silas has

_____. But Silas won't tell Mary _____.

He says that he will _____ the meadow for Warren,

and _____ the pasture, too.

Silas has met _____ _____, a boy who

_____worked___ for Warren for _____several_____

____years____. Silas wants to ____lay____ with Harold

____again____, but Harold is now a ____teacher____. Silas

says that between them they will ____succeed____. Silas wants

another ____chance____ to teach Harold how

____to____ ____pitch____ ____hay____. He hates

to see _____ _____ _____.

This means that _____ _____

_____ _____. Warren is

_____ for Silas because Silas can't look

_____ with _____ or look

_____ with _____. Mary tells Warren that

Silas has come _____ _____

_____. Warren _____ her. They disagree

about the meaning of _____. Warren says,

"_____." Mary

says, "_____." These two

statements show how _____ they are from one

another.

Warren asks about Silas' _____, who is

_____. Why doesn't he _____ his

_____ for _____? Mary knows why: Silas

is _____ and won't be _____

_____. Mary asks Warren to be __*kind*__ to

Silas and not to _____ at him. Silas has come back

with a _____ to _____ Warren.

Warren goes to _____ Silas, and he

_____ very _____. Mary says,

"_____?" and Warren answers, "_____."

STRUCTURE AND STYLE

Connections: Characteristics

1. Which words in the following list belong with Warren, or Mary, or Silas?

   musing   huddled   pity
   kind   pride   broken
   done   undependable   hurt
   nodding off   humble   mocked
   tenderness   changed   nothing
   trouble   worn out   worthless

   Which one of the characters did you connect with many of the preceding words? What do you think the poet is trying to tell us?

2. *Have to*   This expression means *must*. It is used in several places throughout the poem. Who uses it? Where is it used? How is it used?

3. Particles   Sometimes verbs are followed by little words like *in*,
   off, *back*, *on*, *over*, and so on. Frost uses verbs and particles
   throughout the poem. Here is a list of verbs. Find the particles
   that follow them. Do they change the meaning of the verbs?
   How?

drew	pitch
coax	take/takes
come	look(ing)
nodding	goes
ran	had/have

LAST WORDS

Frost never describes the appearance of Warren or Mary. He does
not tell us how they speak. Yet we know them, and we have
feelings about them. Look through the poem again. Find those
lines that tell you the most about the differences between Warren
and Mary.

For example, in line 7, Mary says, "Be kind." In line 12, Warren
says, "But I'll not have the fellow back." And near the end of the
poem in lines 122–125, Warren and Mary describe *home* as they
understand it. They understand *home* differently. What is this
difference?

8
THE MAN WITH THE HOE

Edwin Markham

HEAD NOTES

Edwin Markham (1852–1940) was born into a pioneer family in Oregon. His father had been the leader of a wagon train to the West; his mother wrote poems about her life in this new land. Markham began writing poems after a school teacher introduced him to reading poetry. By this time he and his mother were living on a ranch near San Francisco, California; his father was dead. Markham decided to become a teacher and he taught in a little town in the Sierra Nevada Mountains and later in Berkeley, California. While he was in the mountains, he began his famous poem, "The Man with the Hoe." He wrote the poem in 1899 after seeing a copy of a painting by the same name. The poem was immediately successful, and Markham started a career as a very popular poet and lecturer. When he was eighty years old, a special birthday celebration was held to honor him at Carnegie Hall, a large, famous music hall in New York.

CULTURAL NOTES

The poem without the picture is incomplete. We, too, need to see what the poet was looking at. J. F. Millet was not a famous painter. "The Man with the Hoe" is, however, his most famous painting. Edwin Markham was not a famous poet. But "The Man with the Hoe" is his best-known poem. It appeared in many textbooks in America, and millions of school children read it.

Millet's picture stirred Markham's feelings. In the face and body of Millet's French peasant, Markham sees all the misery of the world. Markham's poem exposes the poet's feelings of anger toward the governments and the rulers who have created "this monstrous thing."

Markham's poem uses language that is "oratorical"—that is, the kind of language that a preacher would use. Markham believes that man was made in the image of God. "The Man with the Hoe" looks like an animal: "a brother to the ox." Markham blames those in power for this poor man. And Markham sees a time when this poor man will rebel against those in power.

STRATEGIES

As you read the poem, these questions will help you to understand it:

What is Markham telling us in the first ten lines?

In lines 11–32 Markham contrasts "The Man with the Hoe" and man made in God's image. What kind of man did God "dream" for the world (lines 11–15)?

How does "The Man with the Hoe" differ from God's image (lines 18–30)?

Whom does Markham blame for "this dread shape?"

What must be done to make a real human being of "The Man with the Hoe" (lines 36–41)?

Markham uses the word "prophecy" (line 32) — a statement of something that will happen. What will happen in "the Future?"

The Man with the Hoe

Edwin Markham

1 *Bowed* by the weight of centuries he leans
2 Upon his hoe and gazes on the ground,
3 The *emptiness of ages* in his face,
4 And on his back the *burden* of the world.
5 Who made him *dead to rapture and despair*,
6 A thing that *grieves not* and that never hopes,
7 *Stolid and stunned*, a brother to the ox?
8 Who loosened and let down this *brutal jaw*?
9 Whose was the hand that slanted back this brow?
10 Whose breath blew out the light within this brain?
11 Is this the Thing the Lord God made and gave
12 To have *dominion* over sea and land;
13 To trace the stars and search the heavens for power;
14 To feel the passion of *Eternity*?
15 Is this the Dream *He* dreamed who shaped the suns
16 And *pillared the blue firmament with light*?
17 Down all the *stretch* of Hell to its last *gulf*
18 There is no shape more terrible than this—
19 More tongued with *censure* of the world's *blind greed*—

---

bowed—bent over; stooped
emptiness of ages—years of misery
burden—load; heavy weight
dead to rapture and despair—unable to feel joy or hopelessness
grieves not—is not sad
stolid and stunned—expressing no feelings
brutal jaw—a jaw like an animal's
dominion—power; rule; control
Eternity—endless time
He—God
pillared the blue firmament with light—made light in the sky
stretch—distance
gulf—a deep place filled with water
censure—blame
blind greed—thoughtless desire to take things

20   More filled with *signs and portents* for the soul—
21   More *fraught with menace* to the universe.

22   What gulfs between him and the *seraphim*!
23   Slave of the wheel of labor, what to him
24   Are *Plato* and the *swing of Pleiades*?
25   What the *long reaches of the peaks of song*,
26   The *rift of dawn*, the reddening of the rose?
27   Through this *dread* shape the suffering ages look;
28   Time's tragedy is in that aching stoop;
29   Through this dread shape humanity *betrayed*,
30   *Plundered, profaned and disinherited*,
31   Cries protest to the Judges of the World,
32   A protest that is also *prophesy*.

33   O masters, lords and rulers in all lands,
34   Is this the handiwork you give to God,
35   This *monstrous* thing *distorted and soul-quenched*?
36   How will you ever straighten up this shape;
37   Touch it again with *immortality*;
38   Give back the upward looking and the light;
39   Rebuild in it the music and the dream;

---

signs and portents—signs of things that will happen
fraught with menace—filled with danger
seraphim—angels
Plato—philosophy
swing of Pleiades—astronomy
long reaches of the peaks of song—great music
rift of dawn—beauty of the sunrise
dread—frightening
betrayed—left in time of need
plundered, profaned and disinherited—robbed, cursed, and left with
   nothing
prophecy—telling of something that will happen
monstrous—like a monster; very ugly
distorted and soul-quenched—twisted and without a soul
immortality—ability to live forever

40 Make right the *immemorial infamies*, terrible thing

Cheating

41 *Perfidious* wrongs, *immedicable woes*?

42 O masters, lords and rulers in all lands,
43 How will the Future *reckon with* this Man?
44 How answer his *brute* question in that hour
45 When *whirlwinds of rebellion* shake the world?

tornado
hurricane

metaphor

RETELLING

Edwin Markham's poem, "_____

_____ _____ _____

_____" was _____ after he

_____ a _____ by the French painter

_____. This _____ shows a French

_____ who _____ like an

_____. This man's _____ made

Markham _____, and his poem _____

his _____ about this poor man's _____.

Markham sees man in _____ image. But the man in

the _____ is a "_____

_____."

---

immemorial infamies — years of evil acts
perfidious — hateful
immedicable woes — miseries that have no cure
reckon with — deal with; judge
brute — rough; cruel; savage
whirlwinds of rebellion — uprisings; revolutions

Markham _____ the "_____,

_____ and _____ in

all _____ " for this "_____

_____." He asks what _____ will do to

_____ back this man's lost _____.

Markham believes that _____ will come to the

_____ in the _____ because of the

_____ done to "_____ _____

_____ _____ _____."

STRUCTURE AND STYLE

Connections: A. Alliteration

English poetry has used alliteration for more than 1,000 years. Alliteration is the repetition of the same initial (first) sound in words. This sound is usually a consonant, and the words are in the same line. For example:

"The sound and smell of the city's streets . . ."

The sound of "s" is repeated four times in this line. ("city's" is spelled 'c' but sounds 's'.)

Which lines in Markham's poem use alliteration? You must find two or more words in each line that begin with the same sound. Write down or underline these alliterative sounds.

Does Markham's poem make use of alliteration rarely? sometimes? often?

Is alliteration important in this poem?

B. Questions

Markham's poem asks questions. The poem has forty-five lines. How many of these lines are questions?

There is a difference between real questions and rhetorical questions. Real questions have answers. Rhetorical questions do not expect answers, because we already know the answer or because the answer is unknown or unnecessary.

Which of Markham's questions are answered in the poem? Write down these questions and their answers.

Which questions are rhetorical?

C. Tone

Markham's style is called *polemic* (or polemical). A polemic piece of writing attacks and blames others. We know whom Markham attacks and blames. The question is: How does he express his polemic (his attack and blame)?

By direction: "O masters, lords and rulers in all lands / You have created a monster / That holds within his hands . . ." etc.

By indirection: "O masters, lords and rulers in all lands / Is this the handiwork you give to God . . ." etc.

Which of these two ways does Markham use most?

D. Diction

Diction is a writer's choice of words. Markham is describing an individual man.

How many different nouns and pronouns does Markham use to describe "The Man with the Hoe?"

E. Parallel Structures

Markham's poem uses structures that are alike in many of his lines. He links these structures together to make the poem move. For example:

". . . he leans / Upon his hoe and gazes on the ground, . . ."

Leans and *gazes* are verbs linked by *and. Upon his hoe and on the ground* are prepositional phrases in parallel. That is, they are structurally the same and they occur in the same place (after the verb).

Here are three questions in parallel. Each one opens a line in the poem.

Who loosened . . .
Whose was the hand . . .
Whose breath . . .

How many other parallel structures can you find in Markham's poem? Underline them or write them down.

Does Markham use parallel structures rarely? sometimes? often?

Is parallelism important in Markham's style?

LAST WORDS

As you know, this poem was written almost 100 years ago.

Was Markham a prophet? What was his vision of "that hour ..."?

If Markham were alive today, whose misery would he write about?

Is there a photograph, picture, or drawing in today's world that has stirred your feelings? What is it?

9

THE CORRESPONDENCE SCHOOL INSTRUCTOR SAYS GOODBYE TO HIS POETRY STUDENTS

Galway Kinnell

HEAD NOTES

See page 11.

CULTURAL NOTES

Americans believe in education. In the U.S. it is possible to go to school or to keep on learning for a long time. There are special programs for people in their sixties and seventies. And there are correspondence schools.

Correspondence schools teach students by mail. Students pay a fee for a course, and the correspondence school sends lessons to the students' homes. Students return their completed assignments to the correspondence school. Their work is read and judged, and perhaps it receives a grade. All kinds of courses are taught by correspondence.

A great many Americans want to become writers. The reasons for this are not clear. Perhaps some people hope to become rich and famous. Some people may be lonely and want to share their thoughts and feelings with others. Whatever their reasons may be, they sign up in large numbers for writing courses.

Teachers in correspondence schools may be regular teachers who want to make extra money. Or they may not be regular teachers at all. A teacher of writing might be a writer who needs to make additional income. Most writers don't earn much money. Neither do correspondence school instructors.

STRATEGIES

Kinnell's poem expresses attitudes and feelings about his work and himself. As you read his "poem, or chopped prose" of thirty-seven lines, let these questions guide you:

The instructor doesn't remember his students by their names. How does he remember them?

What is the instructor's attitude toward his students' work? Does he admire it? Does he make fun of it?

Is he serious about "poisoned glue" or not?

How sincere is he as a teacher?

What is his opinion of his own poem?

Why is he relieved that "it is over?"

In the end, what have his students become for him?

The Correspondence School Instructor Says Goodbye to His Poetry Students

Galway Kinnell

1　Goodbye, lady in *Bangor*, who sent me
2　snapshots of yourself, after definitely *hinting*
3　you were beautiful; goodbye,
4　Miami Beach *urologist*, who enclosed *plain*
5　*brown envelopes* for the return of your very
6　"*Clinical Sonnets*"; goodbye, manufacturer
7　of *brassieres* on the Coast, whose *eclogues*
8　give the fullest treatment in literature yet
9　to the sagging breast *motif*; goodbye, you in *San Quentin*,
10　who wrote, "Being German my hero is *Hitler*,"
11　instead of "Sincerely yours," at the end of long,
12　neat-scripted letters *demolishing*
13　the *pre-Raphaelites*:

14　I swear to you, it was just my way
15　of cheering myself up, as I licked
16　the stamped, self-addressed envelopes,
17　the game I had
18　of trying to guess which one of you, this time,
19　had poisoned his glue. I did care.

Bangor—a city in Maine
hinting—suggesting but not stating directly
urologist—a doctor specializing in problems of the bladder area
plain brown envelopes—envelopes without the sender's name
clinical sonnets—fourteen-line poems in professional detail
brassieres—underclothes to support the breasts
eclogues—nature poems about shepherds
motif—theme; main idea
San Quentin—a state prison in California
Hitler—ruler of Germany, 1933–1945
demolishing—crushing; destroying
pre-Raphaelites—nineteenth-century group of English poets and painters who wanted to bring back the fourteenth-century Italian Renaissance

20 I did read each poem entire.

21 I did say what I thought was the truth

22 in the *mildest* words I knew. And now,

23 in *this poem*, or *chopped prose*, not any better,

24 I realize, than those *troubled lines*

25 I kept sending back to you,

26 I have to say I am *relieved* it is over:

27 at the end I could feel only pity

28 for that urge toward more life

29 your poems kept *smothering* in words, the smell

30 of which, days later, would *tingle*

31 in your nostrils as new, God-given *impulses*

32 to write.

33 Goodbye,

34 you who are, for me the *postmarks* again

35 of *shattered* towns—Xenia, Burnt Cabins, Hornell—

36 their loneliness

37 *given away* in poems, only their *solitude* kept.

---

mildest—kindest; gentlest
this poem—"The Correspondence School Instructor Says Goodbye to His Poetry Students"
chopped prose—prose made to look like poetry
troubled lines—poems that his students wrote
relieved—grateful; glad
smothering—killing or making unconscious by lack of air
tingle—burning feeling in your nose
impulses—sudden motions; desires
postmarks—post office mark, showing place and time a letter was mailed
shattered—small and separate places
given away—described; shown
solitude—isolation; being apart from others

RETELLING

The correspondence school's _____ receives

_____ from all _____ of

_____. They _____ about

_____ of _____: a _____

from Miami wrote "_____ _____"; a

manufacturer on the Coast wrote _____ about

_____ _____; and a lady from

_____ didn't write poems at all: she sent

_____ of _____.

The instructor is _____ by his _____,

but he is _____, too. He has _____ all

their _____ and has tried to _____ them

the _____ about their _____.

He is _____ that it is _____. At the

end, he _____ only _____ for his

students' _____. He says that their _____

keep _____ life in _____. These

_____ have become _____ for him—not

people. He is _____ to _____.

STRUCTURE AND STYLE

Connections: A. Between *Goodbyes*

The poem begins and ends with *goodbye* (which is a shortened form of "God be with you"). Lines 14–32 lie in between the goodbyes. In these lines, the poet/instructor presents three attitudes to us.

1. He wants his students to take him seriously. Which lines tell us of his attempts to be sincere?

2. He also jokes with his students. What is the game he plays?

How do you understand the "poisoned glue" line? Does he think his students want to kill him? Does he want to die because he hates his work? How would these ideas "cheer him up?"

3. Finally, the instructor is honest with his students about his work and their work. Which lines tell us his opinion of his own work? Which lines tell us his judgment of their work?

He tells us of "that urge toward more life your poems kept smothering in words." What do his students' poems do to life? What is the smell then? How did the smell affect his students?

B. Pronouns

Kinnell's poem is direct and personal. It is spoken to his students. We, as readers, are allowed to read it. We "overhear" his goodbye poem. How does Kinnell make his poem direct and personal?
Study his use of pronouns throughout the poem. Which ones does he use over and over?

LAST WORDS

At the end of his poem, Kinnell's students are again postmarks. The towns he names are all small ones: American towns that most people have never heard of.

What is the difference between *loneliness* and *solitude*?

Who gave away loneliness?

Who or what kept solitude?

III

LOVE

10

A VALEDICTION: FORBIDDING MOURNING

John Donne

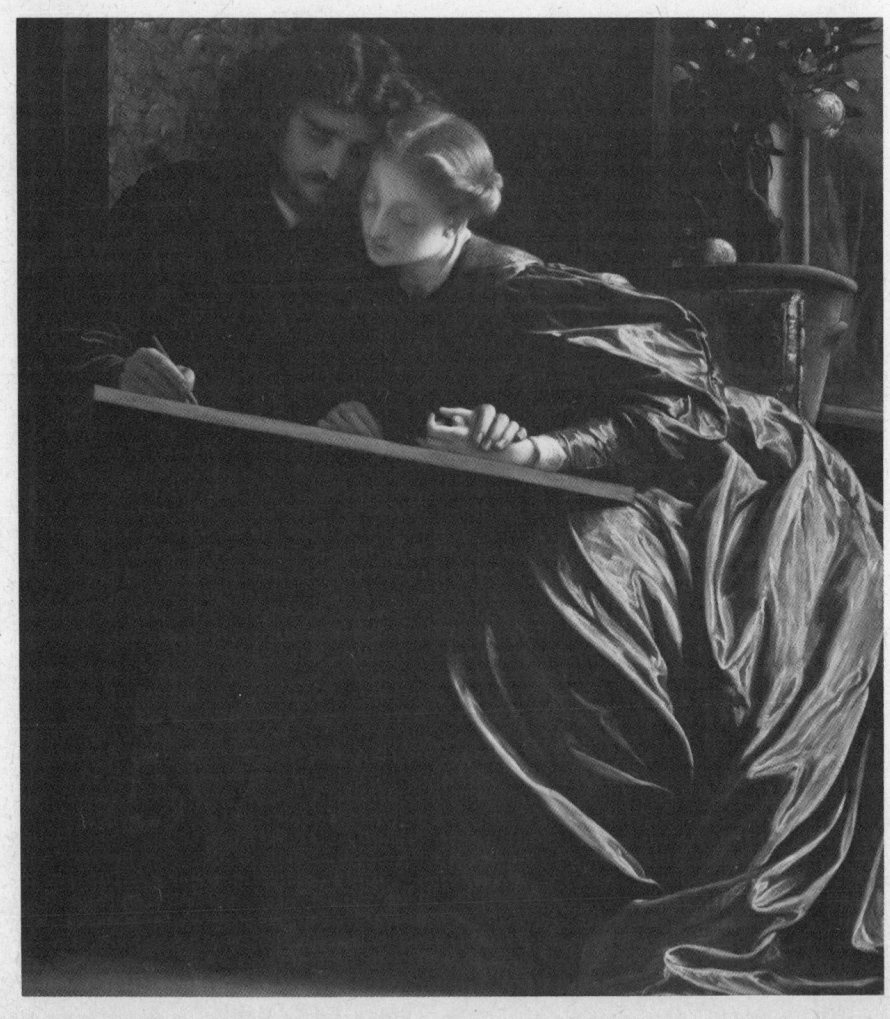

HEAD NOTES

John Donne (1572–1631) and William Shakespeare (1564–1616) were contemporaries; they lived and worked in London at the same time. Both men were poets. But Shakespeare became "the first poet in the English language" and a great dramatist, as well. Donne was generally ignored until the twentieth century, when modern poets "discovered" him and revealed his greatness as a poet.

Donne experienced a number of misfortunes in his life. He became an Anglican (Church of England) priest in 1615. In 1621, he became dean of St. Paul's Cathedral in London, a very important position that he held until his death. Most of his life was a struggle against poverty.

CULTURAL NOTES

Like Shakespeare, Donne was a dramatic poet, but he was not a dramatist. Donne wrote poetry about a wide range of subjects. He was a religious man, a priest, and a preacher, and he wrote sermons and "holy sonnets." But he also wrote tender love poetry. The language Donne used has the sound of everyday speech, and he was a master at combining thought and feeling in his poetry. Perhaps his greatest skill is the creation of *conceits*: metaphors that control an entire poem or a part of it. "A Valediction: Forbidding Mourning" contains such a metaphor, extended to become a conceit.

In Donne's time, the English Renaissance, people believed that the sun revolved around the earth. They also believed that floods and earthquakes happened because the "spheres" (planets) were "out of tune" or "out of order." God had created a perfect world, and people were terribly afraid of change and disorder, or "chaos," as they called it: signs that the world was coming to an end.

Love was of two basic kinds: physical and spiritual. Physical love was ordinary and sensual (of the senses). Spiritual love was extraordinary and pure; it was related to the soul and to angels. Beasts could experience physical love. Spiritual or soulful love overcame these animal passions. Donne contrasts these two kinds of love in his poem.

STRATEGIES

Stanza 1

Donne creates a "mood." He speaks of dying: "pass away," "souls," "whisper," and "breath."

How does Donne take this mood into the second stanza? *So let us melt*

How should "we" be like "them?" *virtuous*

Stanza 3

Donne compares the events of earth and heaven.

Which events are greater? *The events in heaven*

Which events are harmful? *earth*

Which events are innocent? *in heaven*

Stanzas 4 and 5

earthly
sublunary love
the love of senses

refined love
pure

Donne compares two kinds of love.

Which love is physical in nature? Which words tell you this?

Which love is spiritual in nature? Which words tell you this?

Which love do Donne and his wife possess? *Spiritual, (refined)*

Stanza 6

Donne deals with the separation of "Our two souls therefore, which are one . . . ."

How does a "breach" differ from an "expansion?"

How does Donne describe the "expansion?"

Stanzas 7, 8, and 9

Donne uses the carpenter's compass as an extended metaphor: a conceit. *hiding*

Who is the "fixed foot?"

Who is the "running" foot?

What quality in the fixed foot brings the running foot home?

her firmness
(fixed foot)

A *Valediction*: Forbidding *Mourning* *

John Donne

1   As virtuous men pass mildly' away,
2   And whisper to their souls to go,
3   Whilst some of their sad friends do say
4   "The breath goes now," and some say, "No":

5   So let us melt, and make no noise,
6   No tear-floods, nor sigh-tempests move,   *Storm*
7   'Twere *profanation* of our joys
8   To tell the *laity* our love.

distruction
9   *Moving of th' earth* brings harms and fears   *afraid*
wonder
10   Men *reckon* what it did and meant;
11 But *trepidation of the spheres*,
12   Though greater far, is *innocent*.

Dum, Stupid
13 Dull *sublunary* lovers' love   *luna = moon*
(*latin*)
14   (Whose soul is sense) cannot *admit*   *survive*
15 Absence, because it doth remove
16   Those things which *elemented* it.

midst = among us

valediction — farewell; leave-taking
mourning — grief; sorrow
profanation — abuse of something sacred
laity — ordinary people
moving of the earth — an earthquake
reckon — consider
trepidation of the spheres — trembling of the planets
innocent — harmless
sublunary — "under the moon"; earthly
admit — accept; allow
elemented — made (of elements or parts)

*The author of this poem has deleted certain letters and replaced them with apostrophes for purposes of meter.

laity = laiman

17　But we, by' a love so much *refined*

18　　That our selves know not what it is,

19　*Inter-assured of the mind,*

20　　Care less, eyes, lips, and hands to miss.

21　Our two souls therefore, which are one,

22　　Though I must go, *endure* not yet

23　A *breach*, but an *expansion*,

24　　Like gold to airy thinness beat.

Seperation

expansion
(growing may be thinner but longer)

25　If they be two, they are two so

26　　As stiff twin compasses are two;

27　Thy soul, the *fixed* foot, makes no show

28　　To *move*, but doth, if th' other do.

does

29　And though it in the center sit,

30　　Yet when the other far doth *roam*,

31　It leans and *hearkens* after it,

32　　And grows *erect*, as that comes home.

will you

33　Such wilt thou be to me, who must

34　　Like th' other foot, *obliquely run*;

35　Thy firmness makes my circle just,　*Complete, perfect*

36　　And makes me end where I begun.

---

refined — pure
inter-assured of the mind — understanding each other
endure — undergo; suffer
breach — break; gap
expansion — enlargement; increase
fixed — not moving
move — go (physical); feel (spiritual)
roam — travel
hearkens — pays attention to
erect — upward (spiritually)
obliquely — indirectly
run — act; behave

RETELLING

Usually, when lovers ___*love*___ each other, it is a time

of ___*joy*___. Donne speaks of this ___*kind*___ of

___*love*___ as ___*physical*___ love. In his

___*poem*___ to his ___*wife*___, Donne describes

their ___*love*___ as ___*pure*___, and says that their

two ___*souls*___ are ___*one*___. Therefore their

___*separation*___ is not a ___*break*___ but an

___*expansion*___. Donne uses the metaphor of the

___*compass*___ to ___*describe*___ their two

___*souls*___. There is a ___*fixed*___

___*foot*___ and a ___*moving*___ ___*foot*___.

One remains ___*fixed*___ while the other

___*moves*___. Donne describes his ___*wife*___ as the

___*fixed*___ ___*foot*___, while he is the

___*moving*___ ___*foot*___. It is the ___*firmness*___

of his wife's ___*love*___ that ___*brings*___ him

___*home*___.

"Parting is such sweet sorrow"

William Shakespeare

STRUCTURE AND STYLE

Connectors and Their Meanings

Meaning is the most difficult part of language study. A simple way
to separate one kind of meaning from another is by contrast. We
understand the meanings of words like *dog*, *run* and *shoot* in two

ways: (1) by their reference to the "real world" around us; and (2) by their use in sentences.

"My dog has fleas" contrasts with "Your car is a dog" (i.e., no good). "The trains run on time" contrasts with "He hit a home run" or "They run a small store." "Police shoot criminals" contrasts with "Photographers shoot pictures." Many words in English have a range of meanings; we can't talk about *a* meaning or *the* meaning of a word until we hear or see it in context: in a sentence. We can't understand its meaning until its reference to the real world is clear to us.

There are thousands of nouns and verbs that refer to the real world in many ways. But there are only a few connectors: words that join sentences (clauses) and parts of sentences (words and phrases) together. The meaning of connectors is *what* they do in sentences.

John Donne's poem, "A Valediction: Forbidding Mourning," is an argument. The speaker (poet) tries to pursuade his lover that ideal love is rare and beautiful. It is superior to physical, changeable love. How does Donne construct his argument?

He depends on four kinds of meaning expressed by connectors:

The meaning of time

The meaning of contrast

The meaning of possibility

The meaning of result

The connectors that Donne uses to express these meanings are: *as, when, whilst, but, yet, if, though, so, therefore*.

To see how Donne constructs his argument, please read the poem again.

Underline the connectors.

Examine the sentences in which the connectors are used.

Match the connectors and their sentences with the four meanings listed above.

Which connectors did not match easily with the four meanings?

Do you need to enlarge the list of meanings? If so, what meanings would you add to the list?

LAST WORDS

A carpenter's compass is used to draw circles. One "foot" of the compass has a sharp point of metal. The other "foot" contains a pencil that draws the circle.

In Donne's time, the seventeenth century, the circle was the symbol of perfection. A circle with a dot in the center was the symbol for gold. How do these two symbols contribute to the idea of spiritual (soulful) love in the poem?

11

MOTHER
AND
SON

Liam O'Flaherty

HEAD NOTES

Born in the tiny Aran Islands off the west coast of Ireland, Liam O'Flaherty (1896–1984), a major Irish novelist, wrote about the people he saw every day—simple farm people trying to succeed with only poor land and bad weather. Between 1923 and 1950 he wrote fourteen novels and twenty-two other kinds of books. O'Flaherty was active in politics and was forced to leave his country because of his beliefs. He moved to England and began to write. He always wrote about old traditions that have failed. *Famine*, his most famous novel, is about the potato famine during the 1840s when over 1,000,000 Irish died of hunger. He is considered a novelist of the Irish Revolution.

CULTURAL NOTES

The setting for "Mother and Son" is a village in Ireland. The story itself is almost without a plot. That is, there is very little action. There are only two real events: the boy's late return from school and the story he tells his mother. But "Mother and Son" is filled with contrastive feelings: conflicts of emotion. Thus, the main action of the story is psychological, not physical.

Although mother and son are the only characters present, the absent father is also a character we must consider. He is the authority in the family. He punishes the boy when he breaks the rules.

The boy and his mother have a special relationship. "Mother and Son" is about that relationship.

STRATEGIES

Think of this story as a scene from a play, and let these questions guide your reading:

What time is it?

Why is the mother "nervous?"

She has conflicting feelings. What are they?

How does the boy, Stephen, feel as he enters the yard of his house?

Why can't Brigid, the mother, beat her son?

How does she threaten him?

Why was Stephen late coming home from school?

What does he make his mother promise?

What did Stephen see?

How does his mother act after Stephen tells her his story?

Mother and Son

Liam O'Flaherty

1   Although it was only five o'clock, the sun had already set and the evening was very still, as all spring evenings are, just before the birds begin to sing themselves to sleep; or maybe tell one another bedside stories. The village was quiet. The men had gone away to fish for the night after working all the morning with the *sowing*. Women were away milking the cows in the little fields among the *crags*.

2   Brigid Gill was alone in her *cottage* waiting for her little son to come home from school. He was now an hour late, and as he was only nine years she was very *nervous* about him, especially as he was her only child and he was a wild boy, always getting into mischief, *mitching from school*, fishing *minnows* on Sunday and building stone "castles" in the great crag above the village. She kept telling herself that she would give him a good *scolding* and beating when he came in, but at the same time her heart was thumping with anxiety and she *started* at every sound, rushing out to the door and looking down the winding road, that was now dim with the shadows of evening. So many things could happen to a little boy.

3   His dinner of dried fish and roast potatoes was being kept warm in the oven among the peat ashes beside the fire on the *hearth*, and on the table there was a plate, a knife and a little *mug full of buttermilk*.

---

sowing – planting grain
crags – cliffs; steep rocks
cottage – small house
nervous – worried
mitching from school – being absent without permission (dialect)
minnows – small fish
scolding – angry talk
started – jumped up
hearth – fireplace
mug full of buttermilk – a rich, sour milk in a small cup

4   At last she heard the glad cries of the schoolboys afar off, and rushing out she saw their tiny forms *scampering*, not up the road, but across the crags to the left, their caps in their hands.

5   "Thank God," she said, and then she *persuaded* herself that she was very angry. Hurriedly she got a small dried *willow rod*, sat down on a chair within the door and waited for her little Stephen.

6   He *advanced* up the yard very slowly, walking near the stone fence that *bounded* the vegetable garden, holding his *satchel* in his left hand by his side, with his cap in his right hand, a red-cheeked slim boy, dressed in close-fitting grey *frieze* trousers that reached a little below his knees and a blue sweater. His feet were *bare* and covered with all sorts of mud. His face *perspired* and his great soft blue eyes were popping out of his head with fright. He knew his mother would be angry.

7   At last he reached the door and, holding down his head, he entered the kitchen. The mother immediately jumped up and seized him by the shoulder. The boy screamed, dropped his satchel and his cap and *clung to her apron*. The mother raised the rod to strike, but when she looked down at the little trembling body, she began to tremble herself and she dropped the stick. Stooping down, she raised him up and began kissing him, crying at the same time with tears in her eyes.

8   "What's going to become of you *atall, atall*? God save us, I haven't the courage to beat you and you're breaking my heart with your wickedness."

9   The boy sobbed, hiding his head in his mother's *bosom*.

10   "Go away," she said, *thrusting* him away from her, "and eat your dinner. Your father will give to you a good *thrashing* in the morning. I've *spared you*

---

scampering—running quickly
persuaded—convinced
willow rod—a stick made of willow tree wood
advanced—walked forward
bounded—enclosed; surrounded
satchel—a bag for carrying books and papers
frieze—heavy wool
bare—without shoes
perspired—sweated
clung to her apron—held on to her clothing
atall—finally (dialect)
bosom—breast
thrusting—shoving; pushing
thrashing—beating
spared you—saved you (from beating)

often and begged him not to beat you, but this time I'm not going to say a word for you. You've my heart broken, so you have. Come here and eat your dinner."

11   She put the dinner on the plate and pushed the boy into the chair. He sat down sobbing, but presently he wiped his eyes with his sleeve and began to eat *ravenously*. *Gradually* his face brightened and he moved about on the chair, settling himself more comfortably and forgetting all his fears of his mother and the thrashing he was going to get next morning in the joy of satisfying his hunger. The mother sat on the doorstep, *knitting* in silence and watching him lovingly under her long black eyelashes.

12   All her anger had *vanished* by now and she felt glad that she had thrust all the responsibility for punishment on to her husband. Still, she wanted to be *severe*, and although she wanted to ask Stephen what he had been doing, she tried to *hold her tongue*. At last, however, she had to talk.

13   "What *kept you*, Stephen?" she said softly.

14   Stephen swallowed the last mouthful and turned around with his mug in his hand.

15   "We were only playing ball," he said excitedly, "and then *Red Michael* ran after us and chased us out of his field where we were playing. And we had to run an awful way; oh, a long, long way we had to run, over crags where I never was before."

16   "But didn't I often tell you not to go into people's fields to play ball?"

17   "Oh, mother, sure it wasn't me but the other boys that wanted to go, and if I didn't go with them they'd say I was afraid, and father says I mustn't be afraid."

18   "Yes, you *pay heed* to your father but you pay no heed to your mother that has all the trouble with you. Now and what would I do if you fell running over the crags and sprained your ankle?"

---

ravenously — very hungrily
gradually — slowly; after a while
knitting — making cloth from yarn
vanished — disappeared
severe — harsh, strict
hold her tongue — be quiet
kept you — made you late
Red Michael — a farmer
pay heed — listen to; pay attention

19 And she put her apron to her eyes to wipe away a tear.

20 Stephen left his chair, came over to her and put his arms around her neck.

21 "Mother," he said, "I'll tell you what I saw on the crags if you promise not to tell father about me being late and playing ball in Red Michael's field."

22 "I'll do no such thing," she said.

23 "Oh, do, mother," he said, "and I'll never be late again, never, never, never."

24 "All right, Stephen; what did you see, my little treasure?"

25 He sat down beside her on the threshold and, looking *wistfully* out into the sky, his eyes became big and dreamy and his face *assumed an expression of mystery* and wonder.

26 "I saw a great big black horse," he said, "running in the sky over our heads, but none of the other boys saw it but me, and I didn't tell them about it. The horse had seven tails and three heads and its belly was so big that you could put our house into it. I saw it with my two eyes. I did, mother. And then it *soared and galloped* away, away, ever so far. Isn't that a great thing I saw, mother?"

27 "It is, darling," she said dreamily, looking out into the sky, thinking of something with soft eyes. There was silence. Then Stephen spoke again without looking at her.

28 "Sure you won't tell on me, mother?"

29 "No, treasure, I won't."

30 "*On your soul* you won't?"

31 "Hush! little one. Listen to the birds. They are beginning to sing. I won't tell at all. Listen to the beautiful ones."

32 They both sat in silence, listening and dreaming, both of them.

---

wistfully—full of longing and desire
assumed an expression of mystery—became full of mystery
soared and galloped—rose in the air and ran
on your soul—Do you swear . . . ?

RETELLING

_____

Stephen _____ was _____ nine _____

years old, and he was a _____ wild _____ boy. He was

_____ _____ late coming

_____ home _____ from _____ school _____, and his

_____ mother _____ was _____ waiting _____ for him.

_____ Stephen _____ was her _____ only _____ child, and she had

_____ strong _____ feelings _____ she

_____ wanted _____ for him. She was _____ worried _____, but she

was also _____ curious _____. Finally, she made herself

_____ convinced _____ that she was _____ angry _____ at Stephen.

When Stephen _____ entered _____ the _____ yard _____ of his

house, he was _____ frightened _____. He _____ knew _____ that his

mother would be _____ angry _____ because he was

_____ late _____. When Stephen entered

the _____ house _____, his mother _____ grabbed _____ him.

Stephen _____ told _____ his mother and began to

_____ _____. His mother couldn't _____ hear _____ him,

and instead she _____ held _____ him and began to

_____ cry _____ herself.

She _____ pushed _____ him into a _____ chair _____, and

Stephen began to _____ eat _____. Later, she

_____ asked _____ him why he _____ had _____

_____ been _____ so _____ late _____. He _____ told _____

her that he _____ _____ playing

_____ with some other boys. A farmer named

Michael _____ them _____ of his

_____. Stephen _____ over

_____ where he _____ never

_____ before.

Stephen _____ something on the

_____. He made his mother _____ not

to _____ his father what he _____.

Finally, she _____, and Stephen told her about a

_____ _____ with _____

_____ and _____ _____ and

a _____ belly. _____ of the other boys

_____ what Stephen _____.

Stephen's _____ was _____ by his

_____, and they _____ together

_____ to the birds _____.

STRUCTURE AND STYLE

Connections: A. Ambivalence

Psychologists tell us that when we have two conflicting feelings at the same time, we are *ambivalent* ('ambi-'—two; '-valentia'—power, strength). O'Flaherty builds his story on ambivalence, on contrastive feelings.

For example, in the second paragraph of the story, "... she would give him a good scolding and beating when he came in, but at the same time her heart was thumping with anxiety...", Brigid Gill, Stephen's mother, feels the desire to punish him. At the same time she is very worried about his safety: "So many things could happen to a little boy."

Where do you find ambivalence in the rest of the story? Write down or underline those lines that show ambivalent feelings. (The words *but* and *still* may help you to find examples.)

B. Participles (Verb + -*ing* forms) as Modifiers

In the poem, "To Christ Our Lord," by Galway Kinnell, we discovered how verb + -*ing* forms (participles) modified nouns. O'Flaherty makes frequent use of the same structure and pattern.

Here is a brief list of participles that O'Flaherty uses in "Mother and Son." Separate the list into two groups, one for mother and one for son:

waiting
getting (into mischief)
mitching (from school)
rushing
looking

How many others can you find? List them under *mother* or *son*.

How much information do these participles give us about the feelings of mother and son? a little? some? quite a lot?

How important are these participles in O'Flaherty's style?

LAST WORDS

Dialect

Most of O'Flaherty's story uses regular English. But sometimes his two characters speak "Irish-English," a dialect of regular English. A dialect differs from the standard variety of English. This includes variations in vocabulary as well as structures. Mark Twain's novel *Huckleberry Finn*, for example, uses several different dialects to tell the story.

Writers use dialect to make their work seem true and real: *authentic*. O'Flaherty uses just enough dialect to make his characters sound Irish and not English.

In paragraphs 2, 8, 9, 14, 16, and 17 you will find examples of Irish dialectal usage. Write them down or underline them.

How does this use of English differ from standard English? different structure? different words?

12

CRESS DELAHANTY: SPRING

Jessamyn West

HEAD NOTES

Jessamyn West (1907–1984) was a teacher, an editor, a poet, a novelist, and a short story writer. She is best known for her novels and stories about Quaker life in the United States in the nineteenth century. She and her family were Quakers, members of a very small Protestant religion which considers truth and good deeds very important in daily life. Her stories are often about love and courage and a happier time in the past. She is considered a "local color" author because she always gave very specific details about people living in particular places. Her collection of short stories, *Friendly Persuasion*, was made into a movie.

CULTURAL NOTES

Cress Delahanty is a novel about a young woman and her family and friends. The novel describes Cress as she grows up, physically and emotionally, during her adolescence, her teenage years. Cress is an only child; she has no brothers and sisters. She lives in southern California.

As we meet her for the first time, Cress is a fifteen-year-old high school student. She is having an imaginary conversation with her mother. Cress thinks what she says. She doesn't speak to her mother; she speaks to herself and to us, using this "internal monologue."

What is she talking about? The history of love in her young life; the boys and the man who have stirred her feelings as she has grown up. The period of time that she remembers is about ten years: from childhood to mid-adolescence.

STRATEGIES

Cress's memories are a series of names, events, and comments. The series moves chronologically: from her earliest love to her latest one. Two matters are of interest as she tells her story: (1) What happened or is happening as she remembers her experiences? (2) What do we learn about Cress? What kind of person was she and is she?

These questions will help you to understand those two matters:

1. In the "hat scene" with Tommy Fitzgerald, Cress tells a lie to Tommy. What is the lie? Is it a serious or important lie? Why does she do it?

2   When Cress was nine years old, she loved Hubert Fairchild, who was fourteen. What happened to Hubert when he was fourteen? Cress "cried and cried" over Hubert. Why?

3   Cress does things "now" to "suggest things" to boys. What does she do?

4   Cress says, "I'm fifteen. I'm in love." Why does she go to track meets?

5   Cress says that she won't tell who "he" is because Mrs. Agnew (her family's neighbor) will say it's "puppy love." Does she tell who "he" is? Who is he?

6   Cress believes that she is "special" for Mr. Cornelius. Why does she believe this?

7   Why is Mr. Cornelius's illness so important to Cress? What would she like to do for him?

Cress Delahanty: Spring

Jessamyn West

1   We had both been brought to a party and we stood by the bed where our mothers' hats were laid.

2   Tommy said, "That's my mother's hat. It cost $2.98." He was proud of it, he thought it was beautiful, and even I, at five, knew that a $2.98 hat was cheap and that whatever it had cost, Mrs. Fitzgerald's hat was not pretty. It was made of varnished straw and the flowers were of materials not pleasant to see or touch, faded and *flimsy* already, though it was new. It even smelled cheap.

3   "Which is your mother's hat?" Tommy asked.

4   I showed him. It was *lavender*, trimmed with *lilacs* deeper in color and more *velvety* than real lilacs, and it had a *silky veil caught up with a pin* with a real moonstone in it.

5   "How much did it cost?" Tommy asked.

---

flimsy—poorly made; falling apart
lavender—a light purple color
lilacs—lavender-colored flowers
velvety—like the material velvet, soft to the touch
silky veil caught up with a pin—a net hanging in front, held by a long pin
    with a jewel in it

6   It had cost ten dollars, but I heard the *ashamed note* in Tommy's voice. Had he *praised* something silly?

7   "*Just the same*," I said. That, somehow, seemed less of a lie than to say the *round figures*.

8   Tommy was relieved. He gave a snap with thumb and forefinger to the flowers of both hats—to show how unimportant hats—and mothers—and money were. "$2.98? I guess that's the regular price?" he said.

9   I *nodded another lie*. Why? Because I loved Tommy. When we moved to Tenant he gave me a ring with a blue forget-me-not for a *setting*. I still have it. I still remember Tommy. I still remember that lie.

10   When we moved to Tenant, I was nine years old and in the fifth grade. Do you remember Hubert Fairchild, Mother? The kids called him Bert, but I never did. He's dead now. He died during the war, but when I was nine he was fourteen and in the eighth grade, and planning to be a minister. Maybe he was an awful *sissy*—I don't know. He came to school late, because he'd had *typhoid* that summer—and his head was shaved because during the fever most of his hair had fallen out. But I thought he was beautiful and *spiritual* and I loved him.

11   I loved him so much that I hid my face in my desk and cried and cried. Do you know why, Mother? Because he had been sick and in pain and I hadn't been there to nurse him. All that summer while I'd been *carefree*, going to the beach and the mountains, he'd been suffering. It broke my heart. Really I thought it did. So I cried and cried. I told you about it. You thought I should be a Red Cross nurse because I was so *tender-hearted*. I told you as clearly as I could, but you wouldn't believe a word I said. I cried and *moped* and you thought it was sickness and suffering that made me unhappy. It wasn't. It was Hubert.

---

ashamed note—sound of shame
praised—said he admired
Just the same—the same price ($2.98)
round figures—about three dollars
nodded another lie—nodded my head to mean *yes*
setting—ornament; piece of decoration
sissy—a boy who acts like a girl
typhoid—a serious illness that produces high fever
spiritual—sensitive; religious
carefree—without cares
tender-hearted—sympathetic; affectionate
moped—acted sad

12   And now? *Debating*? Because Calvin Dean was on the team last year. In *assembly*, do you know why I sit with my arm around the back of the seat of the girl next to me? Because of the boys in the row behind us. To suggest things to them. Yes, I do. Don't argue, don't *contradict*. I know. I'm the one who does it. And sometimes when I ride into town with Father at *dusk*, do you know what I do? I sit close to him so people will perhaps think he's a *date*. Once, a kid did. He asked me about him the next day. "Who was the guy I saw you out with last night?" he asked.

13   And track meets? Oh, Mother! "*Mad about* track meets." What do I care now about track meets? All that running and jumping and *sawdust pits* and high and low *hurdles*? Nothing, except that he is always there. But if I tell you and Mrs. Agnew, you won't believe it; you'll say I *don't know my own mind*, or what I'm talking about. You'll say, if you do believe it, it's *puppy love* and too silly to talk about. And I won't talk about it. But how else can a puppy love – except like a puppy? He can't be grown up. Or a tiger or a *python*.

14   I'm fifteen. I'm in love. I won't tell you a word about it. But don't be dumb, Mrs. Agnew, just because I wear a *plaid skirt* and am a *yell leader*. The way I act and the way I feel are two different things. And don't think, Mother, just because he's sick too that I ought to be a *Gray Lady* or something.

15   I had heard about him before, but when I saw him I didn't know who he was. He was always at the track meets, dark and slender and *burning-faced*. He stood very straight when he walked, but he always walked toward something, something to lean against or sit on – the grandstand, a *marker-cart*, a box of Coca-Cola. He watched everything very intently, not just the boys running, but the movement of the glossy new leaves in the walnut

---

Debating – a contest of arguments
assembly – general school meeting that everyone attends
contradict – say the opposite
dusk – early evening
date – boyfriend
mad about – very enthusiastic about
sawdust pits – holes filled with wood chips, used by athletes who jump
hurdles – a wooden frame that athletes jump over
don't know my own mind – don't understand myself
puppy love – young love that is not serious or long lasting
python – a large snake
plaid skirt – here, a sort of uniform worn by many young girls
yell leader – someone who stands before others at athletic contests and
        gets them to cheer for their team
Gray Lady – a volunteer helper in hospitals
burning-faced – with a dark-red face
marker-cart – used to make white lines on the track and field

grove next to the track; or a *meadow lark* on a post. He drank things in, he *tipped the cup of seeing* until he had the last drop. He had to—because he's dying.

16   He is Mr. Cornelius. Now you know who he is. He is the father of the Cornelius boys, the track stars. The boys' names are Norman, Wayne, and Lester. They are thirteen, fifteen, and seventeen years old. Mr. Cornelius is thirty-eight. Yes, he is one year older than Father. His name is Mark. His wife drives one of the school buses. She is heavy, with short curly hair that sticks out from under a cap like a taxi man wears. She looks like a lady general in the Russian army. Mr. Cornelius lives in a little tent-house outside his own house so that he can have more fresh air. It is in the walnut orchard, halfway between his house and the school grounds. We can hear his radio and phonograph when we take *P.E.* He plays music I have never heard before.

17   When I go to the track meets I watch him all the time and by now he knows that I do. He smiles at me, he nods his head, he clapped once, just for me to see, when I did a particularly good *back-flip*, leading yells. *It was silent*—but I saw.

18   We never spoke but once. He said, "Do you know my boys?" I said "Yes." He said, "Do you like track meets?" I told him the exact truth. "Yes, but not for the same reason I used to." He knew then; I know he knew. His eyes, they're *hazel*, deepened and darkened. He said, "What's your name?" I told him. "Crescent Delahanty." He said "I know your father, Crescent. I like him."

19   That is all we ever said to each other. But he knows, I know he knows, I love him. I don't know whether he loves me or not but I know I am special for him. There is a special look he has for me, of tenderness, of lovingness. And not as if I were his daughter, either. It is a different look; he would put his arms around me and kiss me, I know, if I went to him, if I put my cheek to his and said "I love you."

20   *I don't know why he would*, exactly. It's not that I have any *illusions* about being beautiful or *talented* or *glamorous*. Is it that I understand more

---

meadow lark—a bird with a pleasant song
tipped the cup of seeing—tried to see everything
P.E.—Physical Education; exercise classes
back-flip—difficult exercise
It was silent—his clapping was soundless
hazel—greenish brown; light brown
I don't know why he would—why he would hold and kiss her
illusions—false beliefs; imaginary life
talented—creative or artistic; gifted
glamorous—beautiful and exciting

...an anyone else how it is for him to be dying? Is it worse for him because he sees more than anyone else? Because he has more to leave behind, a thousand times as much perhaps as ordinary people? And because he was an athlete too? I've heard about it at school, how many *records he broke* as a boy—so he has to leave swiftness behind and grace and winning? People who have never had those, people who can only half see or half touch or who can only *jogtrot*, not run, and who never hear meadow larks or music, dying can't be so hard for them. Can it? And I know how hard it is for him to leave these things, because I practice all the time being him. I begin when I wake up in the morning by thinking, This may be my last day on earth, because whatever he suffers I want to suffer. I would do anything to save him or to make him happy.

RETELLING

Cress Delahanty's _____ memory is about a

_____ that she _____ to a

_____ year _____ boy named

_____ _____. They were

_____ the _____ of hats, and Cress felt

_____ for Tommy because his _____

_____ was _____. Cress

_____ because she _____ Tommy.

Cress's _____ memory is of _____

_____ who was _____ years

_____ _____ Cress. Cress loved Hubert

_____ he had been _____ with

_____. Cress wished that she _____ been

---

records he broke—best performances he beat (for a new record)
jogtrot—run slowly; jog

_____ to _____ Hubert when he

_____ been _____. She explains that

_____ and _____ hadn't made her

_____. It was _____.

Now Cress wants to _____ things to

_____. She _____ in assembly with her

_____ on the _____ of the

_____ next to _____. She

_____ close to her _____ in his

_____ so that people will _____ her

father is a _____.

But her real _____ is _____

_____, who is _____, with three

_____, and is _____ _____

years _____. _____ than Cress's

_____. Mr. Cornelius is _____. He

_____ with difficulty, and he _____

everything very _____.

Cress has _____ to Mr. Cornelius only

_____, but she thinks he _____ that she

_____ him. He has a special _____ for

Cress—of _____. She feels that she

_____ him _____ _____

anyone else. He has _____ to _____

behind _____ other people have, because he was

an _____. It is _____ for him to

_____ the _____ of the world. Cress

wants to _____ whatever he _____, and

most of all, she _____ to_____ him or

to _____ him _____.

STRUCTURE AND STYLE

Connections: A. *Why?/Because* (Colloquial Style)

A colloquy is a conversation. Colloquial style is conversational. It
imitates the way people talk; its language is familiar and informal.

Cress Delahanty's imaginary conversation with her mother is
familiar and informal. Cress is trying to explain her thoughts and
feelings. To do this, Cress uses questions and answers. Usually, she
asks: *Why . . .* ? She answers with *Because . . . .*

How many examples of *Why?/Because* can you find in Cress's
conversation? (Sometimes *Why?* is asked or suggested by other
structures.) Write down these examples or underline them.

Do you believe that the writer's use of *Why?/Because* is an
important structure in her style? Why?

B. The Use of *But* (On the Contrary)

Cress's imaginary conversation with her mother is sometimes like
an argument. It has this design: you (mother) think this . . . , *but*
you're mistaken. Then Cress explains her thoughts and feelings.

How often does Cress use *but* in her "internal monologue?"
Where does she use it? Why? Write down or underline the
examples of this usage.

How important is this usage in the writer's style? What does its
usage tell you about Cress?

C. The Uses of *Know* and *Don't Know*

Cress uses the verb *know* and its negative form *don't know*
eighteen times in her imaginary conversation with her mother.

Find these examples and write them down or underline them.

Do *know* and *don't know* always have the same meaning, or do they have different meanings? How many meanings do *know/don't know* have?

Cress is fifteen years old. Why is it so important for her to know things in this imaginary conversation with her mother?

LAST WORDS

The ways of love are mysterious. We may wonder why people who are so different from each other fall in love. We usually can't know, so we guess.

In the left column is a list of characteristics (attributes) for a young woman. In the right column is a list of characteristics for a young man. These characteristics in the two columns don't match; they don't fit together. And yet this man and woman are in love.

How can you explain this attraction? What would you guess it is?

nineteen years old	twenty-eight years old
dark-haired	blond
short	tall
plump	slender
glamorous	ordinary
talented	intelligent
talkative	quiet
romantic	practical
affectionate	shy
carefree	serious
cheerful	moody

What additional information would you like to have? Why?

13

CRESS DELAHANTY: WINTER

Jessamyn West

Jessamyn West

HEAD NOTES

See p. 115.

CULTURAL NOTES

Cress Delahanty is now several years older, and she has gone away to school. It is a Quaker school. The Quakers, or the Religious Society of Friends, were established in England in the seventeenth century. The term Quaker was first used as an insult by an English judge. Quakers were said to "tremble at the word of the Lord." Quakers believe in peace, racial equality, prison reform, and excellence in education.

Cress attends John Woolman College, named for an eighteenth-century American Quaker. She has a roommate named Edith and a boyfriend named Edwin.

STRATEGIES

Cress has changed. You came to know her as a loving, caring person, when she was fifteen years old. Now she is different, or she seems to be different.

Here are some questions to help you understand Cress:

Why does Cress have to return home?

How does she feel about this?

How does Edwin change her mind?

Why is Cress's father upset by her attitude?

What does she do for her grandfather?

What does Cress's grandfather do for her?

Cress Delahanty: Winter

Jessamyn West

1   Edith shouted from the top of the stairs, "Long distance for you, Cress. *Make it snappy.*"

2   Cress took the stairs *three at a time*, picked up the dangling receiver, pressed it to her ear.

3   "Tenant calling Crescent Delahanty," the operator said. It was her father: "Grandfather is dying, Cress. Catch the 7:30 home. I'll meet you at the depot."

4   "What's the matter—Cressie?" Edith asked.

5   "I have to catch the 7:30 *Pacific Electric*. Grandfather's dying."

6   "Oh poor Cress," Edith cried and pressed her arm about her.

7   Cress hardly heard her. Why are they calling her home to watch Grandpa die, she thought, angrily and rebelliously. An old man, past eighty. He'd never been truly alive for her, never more than a rough, hot hand, a *scraggly* moustache that *repelled* her when he kissed her, an old fellow who gathered what he called "likely-looking" stones and kept them washed and polished, to turn over and admire. It was silly and unfair to make so much of his dying.

8   But before she could say a word, Edith was telling the girls. They were crowding about her. "Don't cry," they said. "We'll pack for you. Be brave, darling Cress. Remember your grandfather has had a long happy life. He wouldn't want you to cry."

9   "Brave Cress—brave Cress," they said. "Just frozen."

10   She wasn't frozen. She was *determined*. She was not going to go. It didn't make sense. She went downstairs to meet Edwin as she had planned, in her green silk, ready for dinner at the *Poinsettia*. The girls had told him.

---

make it snappy—hurry up
three at a time—three steps at a time; quickly
Pacific Electric—an electric train
scraggly—untidy
repelled—made her turn away
determined—definite; decided
Poinsettia—a local restaurant

11   "Are you wearing that home?" he asked.

12   "I'm not going home," she said. "It's silly and useless. I can't help Grandfather. It's just a *convention*. What good can I do him, sitting there at home?"

13   "He might do you some good," Edwin said. "Had you thought of that?"

14   "Why, Edwin!" Cress said. "Why, Edwin!" She had the girls tamed, *eating out of her hand*, and here was Edwin who loved her—he said so, anyway—cold and *disapproving*. Looking at herself through Edwin's eyes, she *hesitated*.

15   "Go on," Edwin said. "Get what you need and I'll drive you to the station."

16   She packed her overnight bag and went with him; there didn't seem—once she'd had Edwin's view of herself—anything else to do. But once on the train her *resentment* returned. The Pacific Electric was hot and smelled of metal and dusty *plush*. It clicked past a *rickety* Mexican settlement, through La Habra and Brea, where the *pool hall* signs swung in the night wind off the ocean. An old man in a spotted corduroy jacket, and his wife, with her hair *straggling* through the holes in her broken *net*, sat in front of her.

17   *Neat*, thought Cress, anyone can be neat, if he wants to.

18   Her father, *bareheaded*, but in his big sheepskin jacket, met her at the depot. It was after nine, cold and *raw*.

19   "This is a sorry time, Cress," he said. He put her suitcase in the back of the car and climbed into the driver's seat without opening the door for her.

---

convention—habit; custom
eating out of her hand—cooperative; agreeable
disapproving—unfavorable; objecting
hesitated—stopped for a moment
resentment—angry displeasure
plush—material covering the seats
rickety—badly built
pool hall—a place where pool is played
straggling—sticking out
net—a covering for the hair
neat—tidy; clean
bareheaded—without a hat
raw—damp

20   Cress got in, wrapped her coat tightly about herself. The sky was clear, the wind had *died down*.

21   "I don't see any sense in my having to come home," she said at last. "What good can I do Grandpa? If he's dying, how can I help?"

22   "I was afraid that was the way you might feel about it. So was your mother."

23   "Oh Mother," Cress *burst out*. "Recently she's always trying to put me . . ."

24   Her father cut her off. "*That'll be about enough*, Cress. Your place is at home and you're coming home and keeping your mouth shut, whatever you think. I don't know what's happened to you recently. If college does this to you, you'd better stay home permanently."

25   There was nothing more said until they turned up the *palm-lined* driveway that led to the house. "Here we are," Mr. Delahanty told her.

26   Mrs. Delahanty met them at the door, tired and *haggard* in her Indian design bathrobe.

27   "Cress," she said, "Grandfather's conscious now. I told him you were coming and he's anxious to see you. You'd better go in right away—this might be the last time he'd know you."

28   Cress was standing by the fireplace holding first one foot then the other toward the fire. "Oh Mother, what am I to say?" she asked. "What can I say? Or does Grandfather just want to see me?"

29   Her father shook his head as if in pain. "Aren't you sorry your grandfather's dying, Cress? Haven't you any pity in your heart? Don't you understand what death means?"

30   "He's an old man," Cress said *obstinately*. "It's what we must expect when we grow old." Though she, of course, would never grow old.

---

died down—almost stopped blowing
burst out—spoke angrily
That'll be about enough—Don't say anything more
palm-lined—planted with palm trees on either side
haggard—suffering
obstinately—stubbornly; refusing to accept her parents' explanation

31   "Warm your hands, Cress," her mother said. "Grandfather's throat bothers him and it *eases him* to have it rubbed. I'll give you the *ointment* and you can rub it in. You won't need to say anything."

32   Cress slid out of her coat and went across the hall with her mother to her grandfather's room. His thin old body was hardly *visible* beneath the covers; his head, with its gray skin and sunken eyes, lay upon the pillow *as if bodiless*. The night light *frosted* his white hair, but made black *caverns* of his closed eyes.

33   "Father," Mrs. Delahanty said. "Father." But the old man didn't move. There was nothing except the occasional hoarse *rasp* of an indrawn breath to show that he was alive.

34   Mrs. Delahanty pulled the cane-bottomed chair a little closer to the bed. "Sit here," she said to Cress, "and rub this into his throat and chest." She opened her father's nightshirt so that an inch or two of bony *grizzled* chest was *bared*. "He says that this rubbing relieves him, even if he's asleep or too tired to speak. Rub it in with a slow steady movement." She went out to the living room leaving the door *a little ajar*.

35   Cress sat down on the chair and put two *squeamish* fingers into the jar of gray ointment; but she could see far more sense to this than to any talking or being talked to. If they had brought her home from school because she was needed in helping to care for Grandpa, that she could understand — but not simply to be present at his death. What had death to do with her?

36   She leaned over him, rubbing, but with eyes shut, dipping her fingers often in the gray grease. The rhythm of the rubbing, the warmth and *closeness* of the room, after the cold drive, had almost put her to sleep when the old man startled her by lifting a shaking hand to the bunch of yellow violets Edith had pinned to the shoulder of her dress before she left Woolman. She opened her eyes suddenly at his touch, but the old man said nothing, only stroked the violets awkwardly with a trembling forefinger.

---

eases him — makes him feel better
ointment — medicine; oily salve or cream
visible — to be seen; noticeable
as if bodiless — not attached to his body
frosted — made white
caverns — holes
rasp — a rough, unpleasant sound
grizzled — gray-colored
bared — uncovered
a little ajar — slightly open
squeamish — unwilling because it's unpleasant
closeness — lack of air

37   Cress unpinned the violets and put them in his hand. "There, Grandpa," she said, "there. They're for you."

38   The old man's voice was a harsh and *faltering* whisper and to hear what he said Cress had to lean very close.

39   I used to—pick them—on Reservoir Hill. I was always sorry to—plow them up. Still—so sweet. Thanks," he said, "to bring them. To remember. You're like her. Your grandmother," he added after a pause. He closed his eyes, holding the bouquet against his face, letting the wilting blossoms spray across one cheek like a pulled-up sheet of flowering earth. He said one more word, not her name but her grandmother's.

40   The *dikes about Cress's heart broke*. "Oh Grandpa, I love you," she said. He heard her. He knew what she said, his fingers returned the pressure of her hand. "You were always so good to me. You were young and you loved flowers." Then she said what was her great discovery. "And you still do. You still love yellow violets, Grandpa, just like me."

41   At the sound of her uncontrolled crying, Mr. and Mrs. Delahanty came to the door. "What's the matter, Cress?"

42   Cress turned, lifted a hand toward them. "Why didn't you tell me?" she demanded. And when they didn't answer, she said, "Edwin knew."

43   Then she dropped her head on her grandfather's outstretched hand and said something, evidently to him, which neither her father nor her mother understood.

44   "It's just the same."

RETELLING

Cress Delahanty _____was_____ away at ___School___

when she ___got___ a ___phone___

___call___ from her ___father___. Cress

___heard___ that her ___grandfather___ was

---

faltering—hesitating; weak
dikes about Cress's heart broke—Cress's self-control was gone and she
   cried

____dying____. At first, she was ____angry____. She had

____never____ really ____liked____ her ____grandfather____,

and she ____disliked____ the idea of ____going____ home

to ____watch____ him ____die____. She

____decided____ not to ____go____, because she

____couldn't____ do him ____any____ ____good____.

But her ____boyfriend____, Edwin, ____changed____ her

____mind____, and they ____drove____ to the

____station____. Cress ____traveled____ home on the

____train____. The ____trip____ took about an

____hour____ and a ____half____.

Cress and her father ____argued____ about her

____coming____ home. Cress's ____mother____ was

____suffering____ and ____told____ Cress that she might

not ____see____ her ____grandfather____ again. Cress agreed

to ____rub____ some ____medicine____ on her

grandfather's ____chest____ and ____throat____, to

____ease____ his ____pain____.

As Cress ____rubbed____ in the ____medicine____, she felt

____sleepy____, but the old man ____woke____ her

____up____ by ____touching____ the bunch of

____flowers____ ____that____ Cress was wearing. He

____spoke____ of Cress's ____grandmother____, and he

____held____ the ____flowers____ against his

____face____. He ____spoke____ one more

_____, and _____ his _____.

Cress _____ into _____, because in

that moment, she _____ that she and her

_____ were very much _____.

_____ had been _____ when he

_____ Cress that her _____ might

_____ her _____ _____.

STRUCTURE AND STYLE

Connections: Speech and Character

1. When Cress was fifteen, she told us about her thoughts and feelings. To do this, she described the boys and the man she loved. She spoke to us as "I," and she is telling her own story. There are other people in the story, and the writer must give each of them a personality and a voice.

   From what Cress's father says, how would you describe his personality?

   How does Cress's mother differ in personality from Cress and her father?

   What is the reason for the dashes (−) between the words that Cress's grandfather speaks?

2. Compare four speeches that Cress makes: to Edwin; to her father in the car; to her mother; to her grandfather.

   How do these four speeches show the changes in Cress's personality?

   Where does she show the least change? the greatest change?

LAST WORDS

Cress's father and mother don't understand what Cress says, "evidently to her grandfather." She says "It's just the same."

What does _it_ refer to?

What is Cress trying to tell her grandfather (and herself)?

IV
DIFFERENCE

14
HARLEM

Langston Hughes

Langston Hughes

HEAD NOTES

Langston Hughes (1902–1967) was a black poet and short-story writer, whose wit and skill turned his anger and despair into literature. His formal education ended when he was nineteen years old. His first collection of poems appeared in 1926, when he was twenty-four. Although he wrote plays, short stories, and autobiographical work, Hughes will probably be remembered most of all for his poetry. In 1960, Hughes received the Spingarn Medal for his writing. This gold medal is awarded each year by the National Association for the Advancement of Colored People to the black person who has achieved greatness in his or her work during the year or over a period of time. Other famous black Americans who have received the Spingarn Medal include Jackie Robinson (baseball), Martin Luther King, Jr. (civil rights), Duke Ellington (music), and Sammy Davis, Jr. (entertainment).

CULTURAL NOTES

"Harlem" was originally titled "Helen." It was published in 1951. The 1950s and 1960s were very important years for black Americans. In 1955, Martin Luther King began his struggle for equality for black Americans. In 1963, Dr. King led a nonviolent demonstration in Washington, D.C., and he gave his famous speech, "I have a dream. . . ."

Langston Hughes was a part of the struggle for the civil rights of black Americans. But he was a cultural, intellectual figure; Martin Luther King was a political and religious figure. They worked together to create permanent changes in American society.

STRATEGIES

"Harlem" is a short poem that asks five questions. The five questions are rhetorical, as they were in the Markham poem, "The Man with the Hoe." That is, the poem doesn't provide the answers. The reader must answer the questions.

The first question is the basic question. All the other questions are connected to the first one.

If a "dream deferred" dries up "like a raisin in the sun," what happens to the dream in the real world?

If a "dream deferred" *festers* and *runs*, what happens to the dream in the real world?

If it *stinks* and *crusts over*, what happens to it?

If a "dream deferred" *explodes*, what happens to society?

From your knowledge of recent American history, what *did* happen to a "dream deferred?"

Harlem

Langston Hughes

1   What happens to a dream *deferred*?

2   Does it dry up
3   like a *raisin* in the sun?

4   Or *fester* like a sore —
5   And then run?
6   Does it *stink* like rotten meat?
7   Or *crust and sugar over* —
8   like a syrupy sweet?

9   Maybe it just *sags*
10   Like a heavy load.

11   Or does it *explode*?

RETELLING

I'll _____ you what _____

When a ____dream____ is ____delayed____

---

deferred — delayed (in happening)
raisin — dried grape
fester — rot; create poison
stink — smell bad
crust and sugar over — sugar forming a hard surface
sags — hangs down
explode — blow up; burst from pressure within

It ___dries___ ___up___ like a ___raisin___

In the ___sun___

It becomes _____ like a _____

And it _____ like _____

_____

Or it _____ over

Like a _____ _____

Maybe we _____

Under its _____

But one _____

The _____ will _____!

STRUCTURE AND STYLE

Connections: Questions and Statements/Forms and Functions

Rhetorical questions are really statements or answers in the form of questions. The writer knows the answer already. He uses the form of the question to make the reader answer the question, or at least think about the reason for the question.

Compare the questioning style of "Harlem" to the statement version of the poem you wrote in the preceding section. Do you prefer questions or statements? Why?

LAST WORDS

The word *dream* is used by the poet, Langston Hughes, in 1951, and by the black leader, Martin Luther King, in 1963.

What is this dream that both men refer to?

Is this dream a reality today, or is it still "deferred?"

15
FEAST

Eric Larsen

HEAD NOTES

Eric Larsen is a young writer who lives and teaches in New York City. "Feast" was first published in the South Dakota *Review* in the Autumn of 1971.

CULTURAL NOTES

"Feast" takes place in a rural elementary school; the season is winter. We don't know the location of the school. However, from the description of the teacher's clothing and the presence of Eskimos, we may guess that the school is near or in Canada.

STRATEGIES

The narrator is a sixth-grade student. We don't know whether the narrator is a boy or a girl. We may guess that the narrator is a boy. He tells us what happens during one December day at school.

As you read "Feast," let these questions guide you:

The narrator tells us "I felt (that Miss Cutter) was an earnest and idealistic young woman." Why does he come to this conclusion about Miss Cutter?

How does the story get its title?

What "treat" does Miss Cutter plan for her class?

How does the class prepare for the Eskimos' visit?

Much of the story is about the snowstorm and what happens as the snow falls. Why is the snowstorm so important?

Do you think that the Eskimo was a child or a woman? What contrastive evidence does the writer give us?

How is the Eskimo different from the narrator and his classmates?

What, exactly, is Miss Cutter trying to show her students by bringing the Eskimo to class?

Do we know how the narrator felt about Miss Cutter's "feast?"

At the end of the story, what seems to be most important to the narrator and his classmates?

Feast

Eric Larsen

1   In the sixth grade I had a teacher whose name was Christine Cutter. Even then I felt she was an *earnest and idealistic* young woman; a *miniature* silver cross hung each day from a fine chain around her neck and she was fond of wearing a blue *blazer* that had the *gold-embroidered emblem* of the college she had graduated from sewn over her left breast. The college was named after one of the female *saints*, and its emblem *depicted* an open book *radiating beams of light* upward toward heaven, which was represented by three *hovering gold clouds*.

2   Miss Cutter felt that learning should be a meaningful experience. She *endeavored* to reveal the excitement of life to us, and to *expand our vision* to the point where we were aware of the great feast of knowledge the world had to offer. She attempted to bring things into the classroom, and she took us *in turn* outside to see things in the world. We went on *outings* to factories and fire departments and courthouses. Once we went to a local dairy, and Miss Cutter was fascinated by seeing the white bubbling milk flowing through *transparent* pipes under the ceiling.

3   Before Christmas she announced a special treat. A group of live Eskimos was to visit the class. We would be able to see them *in the flesh*.

4   The day they were to arrive started out warm and gray. A light mist was falling. By the middle of the morning, from inside the steam-heated classroom, you could see that it was getting thicker; it was starting to form drops and beads as it drifted against the windowpanes. Then it turned to snow, shapeless heavy flakes falling straight down.

---

feast — literally, a big meal; figuratively, anything that gives great pleasure
earnest and idealistic — serious and thoughtful
miniature — small
blazer — jacket
gold-embroidered emblem — sign sewn in gold thread
saints — holy people
depicted — showed
radiating beams of light — sending out rays of light
hovering gold clouds — gold clouds hanging above
endeavored — tried
expand our vision — help us to understand
in turn — also; as well
outings — trips; visits
transparent — clear (glass)
in the flesh — as real people (not as pictures)

5   We ate lunch as usual in a room in the basement that was used the rest of the day as a gymnasium for the lowest three grades. *Suspended* under the ceiling there was a *jungle of steampipes* that made hissing sounds and dropped water down onto the *pressboard tables* that held our meals.

6   In the afternoon the disappointment grew general when it became clear that the visitors were going to be late. We read over the chapter on Eskimos in our book, and Miss Cutter pointed out once more how the women chew on the hides of animals in order to make them soft. As we studied further with bowed heads she *paced* around the room, glancing at the clock and gazing out the steamed windows at the thickly falling snow outdoors. She stood with her arms folded together so that her breasts were like two cats sleeping in a cradle.

7   She gave us *recess* in spite of the snow, and let us stay out longer than usual. It seemed dark outdoors and there was a *peculiar hush* in the air that seemed to *absorb the sound* of our voices and make our shouts sound as though they came from a great distance. The snow was already several inches deep over the ground, and heavy and damp.

8   Some of the girls began building snowmen, and others began games of Fox and Goose. The boys had a game of what we called Victim. Each of us chose a victim and attempted to *bring him down* in the snow. Everyone was a victim and a chaser at once, although the swiftest runners were seldom brought down.

9   Tim Greves was hurt. Someone hit him in the face and he had a bloody nose. He was very small, even for his age, and he *wailed* in surprise and fear. The blood went down his chin and onto his coat until Tracy Cook put her arm around his shoulder and bent down and told him to lean forward. Then the blood dripped onto the snow, and she walked with him into the school with her arm around his shoulder.

10   We *milled around* not knowing what to do. It seemed strange outdoors, growing darker and the snow falling heavily through the hushed air. Tracy

---

suspended—hung
jungle of steampipes—many pipes crossing over one another
pressboard tables—large wooden tables
paced—walked slowly
recess—time to play outside
peculiar hush—strange quiet
absorb the sound—hold and reduce the sound
bring him down—make him fall; tackle him
wailed—cried loudly
milled around—walked around without direction

Cook came back and stood with us. She had light hair and blue eyes, and flakes of snow caught in the lashes of her eyes and *clung* there before they melted.

11   A drop of Tim Greves' blood had fallen on the white fur *cuff* of her coat and she scrubbed at it with snow a moment but then gave up. We were standing by the flag pole and Wendell Cleaver *dared* people to put their tongues on it. It was made of steel and no one would do it. We made a game of trying to see the top of the pole, but the snow fell into your eyes so it was hard to keep them open when you turned your face upward to look.

12   At last Miss Cutter called and we went back inside. It was already the end of the afternoon, and she made us sit down without taking off our coats. It was hot in the room. People's faces were red and *burning*. There was the smell of wet wool in the air.

13   There was only one Eskimo. She was a tiny figure, almost like a doll, *padded and bulky* in *leggings* and *parka* made of brown animal hide *trimmed with fur* at the wrists and the ankles and waist. There was fur around her hood, too, so that her small round face looked out at us from behind a perfect circle of gray fur. Her skin was *weathered* and almost black, soft and *creased* like the leather on the seats of *antique* cars. Her tiny black eyes jumped around the room as though she were afraid.

14   We stared at her.

15   The bell had already rung, but Miss Cutter placed the tiny Eskimo on a chair in the front of the room. Her feet *failed to touch* the floor, and her small brown hands, like paws with their short *stubby* fingers, rested together in her lap. Miss Cutter *squatted down* beside her and showed her how to open her mouth and bare her teeth. She did it herself several times before the

---

clung—stayed; hung; stuck
cuff—part of the sleeve covering the wrist
dared—invited them to take a chance or risk
burning—hot (from exercise outside)
padded and bulky—stuffed and shapeless
leggings—leg coverings
parka—a warm jacket for winter wear
trimmed with fur—with fur sewn on
weathered—rough looking
creased—wrinkled
antique—old
failed to touch—did not touch
stubby—short and thick
squatted down—crouched or sat down

Eskimo understood and opened her mouth up and stretched her lips back with her fingers the way Miss Cutter had done.

16   Then we *filed* past one by one and looked into her face. With her little black eyes *fixed on* us as though in terror, we looked into the *opened privacy of her mouth* to see the way her small teeth were worn down to almost nothing, just rows of *stubs* flattened and worn away down to the gums.

17   After we had seen, we went out of the classroom and into the hallway and out the door of the school again. When I stepped out, it seemed colder than before; after the steaming classroom the air was cold against my heated face, and I met it with relief and breathed it in as if I were thirsty for its coolness.

18   Others came out the door. The snow was still falling, and the air was hushed and growing dark; it would be an early *dusk*. We began running across the snow-covered yard toward where the buses were waiting with their engines running and their small yellow lights shining through the snow. There was the musical *jingle* of the loose *clasps* on our boots as we ran, and one of the drivers called out with a curse that we ought to hurry at that because the roads were already hardly passable and school should have been *cancelled* hours before.

RETELLING

When he was in the _____ grade, the

_____ remembers a _____ day when his

teacher _____ to bring some _____ to

_____ the _____. On the

_____ of that _____ it _____

to _____. By _____, the

---

filed — slowly walked
fixed on — staring at
opened privacy of her mouth — her open mouth
stubs — very short teeth
dusk — evening; the time between light and dark
jingle — musical sound, like bells ringing
clasps — metal buckles
cancelled — here, closed; stopped

_____ and their _____ realized that the

_____ would be _____. The students

_____ about _____ in their

_____, and the teacher _____ them

_____ again about Eskimo _____, who

_____ animal _____ to _____

them _____.

Later in the _____, it _____ to

_____ heavily, but the teacher _____ the

students a _____, so that they could

_____ in the snow. The girls _____ quiet

_____, but the boys' games were _____.

One of the boys _____ a _____

_____.

_____, the teacher _____ the students,

and they _____ to the _____. Inside they

_____ one _____, a _____

woman _____ in _____ and a fur

_____. The teacher _____ the Eskimo

_____ how to _____ her

_____ and _____ her _____.

Then the students _____ past the Eskimo and

_____ inside her _____. Her

_____ were almost _____. She seemed to

be _____ of the students.

Afterwards the students _____ to the

_____ buses that would _____ them

_____.

STRUCTURE AND STYLE

Connections: Contrasts

1. "Feast" is a story that depends on contrasts between what *is* (from the verb *to be*) and what *might be* (from the verbs *to seem*, *to attempt*, and *to feel*; and from the structure words *like*, *as though*, *as if*). The action of the story also depends on what happens or on what doesn't happen. The focus of the story is on the contrast between what is usual and what is unusual or different.

To see how these contrasts work, try making these connections:

What does the narrator (I) *feel* in the first paragraph? Substitute the verb *know* for *feel*. How does the meaning change?

What does Miss Cutter *feel*, *endeavor* (try), and *attempt* in the second paragraph? How would you change these sentences so that they are statements of fact?

In which paragraph is the focus of the story presented? How is it presented (notice the verb forms)?

Snowfall is not unusual to the students in the school. How do we know that they are used to snow and cold weather?

How is the snowstorm on this day unusual (notice the use of *seem*, *as though*, and *as if*)?

Like is used to describe Miss Cutter (paragraph 6) and the Eskimo (paragraphs 13 and 15). How do the comparisons differ?

2. "Feast" also depends on other contrasts. Consider light (whiteness) and darkness.

Find the lines that present these contrasts.

Consider size: big and little

Find the lines that present these contrasts.

Consider hot and cold

Find the lines that present these contrasts.

Of these three sets of contrasts that you have found, which set seems to be the most powerful one? Why do you think so?

LAST WORDS

Miss Cutter wants her students to realize "the great feast of knowledge the world had to offer." Yet when she brings an Eskimo to the classroom, Miss Cutter shows her class only one thing: the Eskimo woman's little, worn down teeth.

When we try to understand people from other cultures, why do we select things that are different?

What were Miss Cutter's students supposed to learn from this experience?

Is "Feast" supposed to be a pathetic story or an amusing one? How did it make you feel?

16
TULARECITO

John Steinbeck

HEAD NOTES

During his youth, John Steinbeck (1902–1968) was a fruit picker and a laboratory helper. He attended Stanford University as a special student. Some of his many novels and stories were written about the Salinas Valley, a beautiful farming region south of San Francisco where he was born and lived. Steinbeck connects the world of nature and the world of people in all his writing. The waste of people's lives and land is one of his frequent themes.

In order to write about the difficult economic times called the Great Depression, Steinbeck went east to Oklahoma and traveled back west with some "Okies." These homeless farm families were coming to California to start new lives. The banks had taken their lands. Steinbeck traveled and lived with them for two years. He wrote about his experiences in *The Grapes of Wrath*, published in 1939, a novel which won him the Pulitzer Prize in 1940.

Many of Steinbeck's works have been made into movies including *The Grapes of Wrath*, *East of Eden*, and *Of Mice and Men*. He was awarded the Nobel Prize for Literature in 1962.

CULTURAL NOTES

"Tularecito" is a long short story. You will read the last part of it. In the first part of "Tularecito" Steinbeck tells us that the setting of the story is in the Salinas Valley in California. The Salinas Valley is a community of farms, orchards, and ranches.

Tularecito ("little frog" in Spanish) is found in the bushes by Pancho, a hired man, who works for Franklin Gomez, a rancher. Pancho was riding back to the ranch one night, and he heard a baby crying. Pancho stopped and searched until he found the baby. It was very ugly, and Pancho named it Tularecito. Someone had left this baby to die; but Pancho was a good man, and he saved the baby's life.

Franklin Gomez took care of Tularecito. As the boy grew up, he became very strong. He could do a man's work when he was nine or ten years old. But his mind did not develop. His mind remained childish and very simple.

Tularecito was a problem when he went to school. He could not learn reading, writing, or arithmetic. However, he had a great gift. He could make beautiful animals out of clay, and he could draw animals with great skill.

Tularecito had a terrible temper. If anyone made fun of his drawings or erased them from the blackboard, Tularecito would fight with them. Because of his behavior, one teacher left the school. Miss Morgan came to replace this teacher. She and Tularecito developed a curious friendship, as you will discover.

STRATEGIES

Here are some questions to help you understand "Tularecito":

Why was Miss Morgan successful in teaching her students?

How did she help Tularecito?

When and why did Tularecito stop drawing and begin listening?

When Miss Morgan writes a letter about "man . . . (leaving) his proof (of existence) on the lives of other people . . ." is she writing about herself, too? Is she explaining why she became a teacher?

Why is Miss Morgan afraid of Tularecito?

Why does Miss Morgan decide to let Tularecito believe in gnomes?

How does Miss Morgan encourage Tularecito to search for gnomes?

Why is Pancho opposed to Tularecito's plan?

Why does Tularecito feel that searching for gnomes is a "homecoming" for him?

What does Tularecito do to find the gnomes?

Why does Bert Munroe spoil Tularecito's work?

Why does Tularecito attack Bert?

Why do the doctors send Tularecito to a mental hospital?

Tularecito

John Steinbeck

1   Miss Morgan, the new teacher, was very young and very pretty; too young and dangerously pretty, the aged men of the valley thought. Some of the boys in the upper grades were seventeen years old. It was seriously doubted that a teacher so young and so pretty could keep any kind of order in the school.

2   She brought with her a breathless enthusiasm for her *trade*. The school was *astounded*, for it had been used to ageing *spinsters* whose *faces seemed to reflect consistently tired feet*. Miss Morgan enjoyed teaching and made school an exciting place where unusual things happened.

3   From the first Miss Morgan was *vastly impressed* with Tularecito. She knew all about him, had read books and taken courses about him. Having heard about the fight, she *laid off a border* around the top of the blackboards for him to fill with animals, and, when he had completed this parade, she bought with her own money a huge drawing pad and a soft pencil. After that he did not bother with spelling. Every day he labored over his drawing board, and every afternoon presented the teacher with a marveously *wrought* animal. She pinned his drawings to the schoolroom wall above the blackboards.

4   The pupils received Miss Morgan's *innovations* with enthusiasm. Classes became exciting, and even the boys who had made *enviable reputations through teacher-baiting*, grew less interested in the possible burning of the schoolhouse.

5   Miss Morgan introduced a practice that made the pupils adore her. Every afternoon she read to them for half an hour. She read by *installments*, Ivanhoe and The Talisman; fishing stories by Zane Grey; hunting stories of

---

trade — profession (teaching)
astounded — greatly surprised
spinsters — unmarried women
faces seemed to reflect consistently tired feet — expressions showed
  that they were tired of standing
vastly impressed — greatly pleased
laid off a border — drew lines
wrought — made; created
innovations — new ideas and activities
enviable reputations through teacher-baiting — had become famous
  for bothering teachers
installments — chapters; sections

James Oliver Curwood; The Sea Wolf, The Call of the Wild—not baby stories about the little red hen and the fox and the geese, but exciting grown-up stories.

6   Miss Morgan read well. Even the tougher boys were won over until they never *played hooky* for fear of missing an installment, until they leaned forward gasping with interest.

7   But Tularecito continued his careful drawing, only pausing now and then to *blink* at the teacher and to try to understand how these distant accounts of the actions of strangers could be of interest to anyone. To him they were *chronicles of actual events*—else why were they written down. The stories were like the lessons. Tularecito did not listen to them.

8   After a time Miss Morgan felt that she had been *humoring* the older children too much. She herself liked fairy tales, liked to think of whole populations who believed in fairies and consequently saw them. Within the safe circle of her *tried and erudite acquaintance*, she often said that "part of America's cultural starvation was due to its *boorish and superstitious denial* of the existence of fairies." For a time she devoted the afternoon half hour to fairy tales.

9   Now a change came over Tularecito. Gradually, as Miss Morgan read about *elves and brownies, fairies, pixies, and changelings*, his interest centered and his busy pencil lay idly in his hand. Then she read about *gnomes*, and their lives and habits, and he dropped his pencil altogether and leaned toward the teacher to *intercept her words*.

10   After school Miss Morgan walked half a mile to the farm where she *boarded*. She liked to walk the way alone, *cutting off thistle heads with a switch*, or throwing stones into the brush to make the *quail roar up*. She thought she should get a *bounding, inquisitive dog* that could share her

---

played hooky—stayed away from school
blink—open and shut his eyes quickly
chronicles of actual events—true histories
humoring—trying to please
tried and erudite acquaintance—trusted and intelligent friends
boorish and superstitious denial—ignorant and frightened refusal
elves and brownies, fairies, pixies, and changelings—magical
    creatures
gnomes—tiny human-like creatures that live underground
intercept her words—catch her words and understand them
boarded—had a room and meals
cutting off thistle heads with a switch—using a stick to destroy plants
quail roar up—birds fly up noisily
bounding, inquisitive dog—an active, curious dog

excitements, could understand the *glamour of holes* in the ground, and scattering pawsteps on dry leaves, of strange melancholy bird whistles and the gay smells that came secretly out of the earth.

11   One afternoon Miss Morgan scrambled high up the side of a *chalk cliff* to carve her initials on the white plane. On the way up she tore her finger on a thorn, and, instead of initials, she scratched: "Here I have been and left this part of me," and pressed her bloody finger against the absorbent chalk rock.

12   That night, in a letter, she wrote: "After the bare *requisites* to living and reproducing, man wants most to leave some record of himself, a proof, perhaps, that he has really existed. He leaves his proof on wood, on stone or on the lives of other people. This deep desire exists in everyone, from the boy who writes dirty words in a public toilet to the *Buddha* who *etches his image* in the *race mind*. Life is so unreal. I think that we seriously doubt that we exist and go about trying to prove that we do." She kept a copy of the letter.

13   On the afternoon when she had read about the gnomes, as she walked home, the grasses beside the road *threshed about* for a moment and the ugly head of Tularecito appeared.

14   "Oh! You frightened me," Miss Morgan cried. "You shouldn't pop up like that."

15   Tularecito stood up and smiled *bashfully* while he whipped his hat against his thigh. Suddenly Miss Morgan felt fear rising in her. The road was deserted—she had read stories of *half-wits*. With difficulty she mastered her trembling voice.

16   "What—what is it you want?"

17   Tularecito smiled more broadly and whipped harder with his hat.

18   "Were you just lying there, or do you want something?"

---

glamour of holes—here, the magic of animal burrows in the ground
chalk cliff—an overhanging rock of soft, white stone
requisites—necessities
Buddha—sixth-century B.C. religious leader
etches his image—creates a picture of himself
race mind—the thought and feelings of human beings
threshed about—moved suddenly
bashfully—shyly
half-wits—people who lack normal intelligence

19   The boy struggled to speak, and then *relapsed* into his protective smile.

20   "Well, if you don't want anything, I'll go on." She was really prepared for flight.

21   Tularecito struggled again. "About those people—"

22   "What people?" she demanded *shrilly*. "About what people?"

23   "About those people in the book—"

24   Miss Morgan laughed with relief until she felt that her hair was coming loose on the back of her head. "You mean—you mean—gnomes?"

25   Tularecito nodded.

26   "What do you want to know about them?"

27   "I never saw any," said Tularecito. His voice neither rose nor fell, but continued on one low note.

28   "Why, few people do see them, I think."

29   "But I knew about them."

30   Miss Morgan's eyes *squinted* with interest. "You did? Who told you about them?"

31   "Nobody."

32   "You never saw them, and no one told you? How could you know about them then?"

33   "I just knew. Heard them, maybe. I knew them in the book all right."

34   Miss Morgan thought: "Why should I *deny gnomes* to this queer, unfinished child? Wouldn't his life be richer and happier if he did believe in them? And what harm could it possibly do?"

35   "Have you ever looked for them?" she asked.

36   "No, I never looked. I just knew. But I will look now."

---

relapsed—went back
shrilly—in a high voice
squinted—narrowed
deny gnomes—say that gnomes don't exist

37 Miss Morgan found herself charmed with the situation. Here was paper on which to write, here was a cliff on which to carve. She could *carve a lovely story* that would be far more real than a book story ever could. "Where will you look?" she asked.

38 "I'll dig in holes," said Tularecito soberly.

39 "But the gnomes only come out at night, Tularecito. You must watch for them in the night. And you must come and tell me if you find any. Will you do that?"

40 "I'll come," he agreed.

41 She left him staring after her. All the way home she pictured him searching in the night. The picture pleased her. He might even find the gnomes, might live with them and talk to them. With *a few suggestive words* she had been able to make his life unreal and very wonderful, and separated from the stupid lives about him. She deeply *envied him his searching*.

42 In the evening Tularecito put on his coat and took up a shovel. Old Pancho came upon him as he was leaving the tool shed. *"Where goest thou,* Little Frog?" he asked.

43 Tularecito shifted his feet restlessly at the delay. "I go out into the dark. Is that a new thing?"

44 "But why takest thou the shovel? Is there gold, perhaps?"

45 The boy's face grew hard with the seriousness of his purpose. "I go to dig for the little people who live in the earth."

46 Now Pancho was filled with *horrified excitement*. "Do not go, Little Frog! Listen to your old friend, your father in God, and do not go! Out in the *sage* I found thee and saved thee from the devils, thy relatives. Thou art a little brother of Jesus now. Go not back to thine own people! Listen to an old man, Little Frog!"

47 Tularecito stared hard at the ground and *drilled his old thoughts* with this

---

carve a lovely story — she would change a person's life
a few suggestive words — a few encouraging words
envied him his searching — wished she could search, too
Where goest thou? — Where are you going?
horrified excitement — frightened worry
sage — sagebrush; bushes
drilled his old thoughts — considered

new information. "Thou hast said they are my people," he exclaimed. "I am not like the others at the school or here. I know that. I have loneliness for my own people who live deep in the cool earth. When I pass a squirrel hole, I wish to crawl into it and hide myself. My own people are like me, and they have called me. I must go home to them, Pancho."

48   Pancho stepped back and held up crossed fingers. "Go back to the devil, thy father, then. I am not good enough to fight this evil. It would take a saint. But see! At least I make the *sign* against thee and against all thy race." He drew the cross of protection in the air in front of him.

49   Tularecito smiled sadly, and turning, *trudged* off into the hills.

50   The heart of Tularecito *gushed with joy* at his homecoming. All his life he had been an alien, a lonely *outcast*, and now he was going home. As always, he heard the voices of the earth—the far-off clang of cow bells, the *muttering of disturbed quail*, the little whine of a *coyote* who would not sing this night, the *nocturnes* of a million insects. But Tularecito was listening for another sound, the movement of two-footed creatures, and the hushed voices of the hidden people.

51   Once he stopped and called, "My father, I have come home," and he heard no answer. Into squirrel holes he whispered, "Where are you, my people? It is only Tularecito come home." But there was no reply. Worse, he had no feeling that the gnomes were near. He knew that a *doe and fawn* were feeding near him; he knew a wildcat was stalking a rabbit behind a bush, although he could not see them, but from the gnomes he had no message.

52   A *sugar-moon* arose out of the hills.

53   "Now the animals will come out to feed," Tularecito said in the papery whisper of the half-witless. "Now the people will come out, too."

54   The *brush* stopped at the edge of a little valley and an orchard took its place. The trees were thick with leaves, and the land finely cultivated. It was

---

sign—sign of the Christian cross
trudged—walked slowly
gushed with joy—filled up with pleasure
outcast—one who doesn't belong to a group
muttering of disturbed quail—sounds of upset birds
coyote—a small wolflike animal
nocturnes—night songs
doe and fawn—mother and baby deer
sugar moon—a large, yellow-colored moon
brush—bushes; low-growing plants

Bert Munroe's orchard. Often, when the land was deserted and *ghost-ridden*, Tularecito had come here in the night to lie on the ground under the trees and *pick the stars with gentle fingers*.

55   The moment he walked into the orchard he knew he was nearing home. He could not hear them, but he knew the gnomes were near. Over and over he called to them, but they did not come.

56   "Perhaps they do not like the moonlight," he said.

57   At the foot of a large peach tree he dug his hole—three feet across and very deep. All night he worked on it, stopping to listen awhile and then digging deeper and deeper into the cool earth. Although he heard nothing, he was positive that he was nearing them. Only when the daylight came did he give up and retire into the bushes to sleep.

58   In midmorning Bert Munroe walked out to look at a coyote trap and found the hole at the foot of the tree. "What the devil!" he said. "Some kids must have been digging a tunnel. That's dangerous! It'll *cave in* on them, or somebody will fall into it and get hurt." He walked back to the house, got a shovel and filled up the hole.

59   "Manny," he said to his youngest boy, "you haven't been digging in the orchard, have you?"

60   "Uh-uh!" said Manny.

61   "Well, do you know who has?"

62   "Uh-uh!" said Manny.

63   "Well, somebody dug a deep hole out there. It's dangerous. You tell the boys not to dig or they'll get caved in."

64   The dark came and Tularecito walked out of the brush to dig in his hole again. When he found it filled up, he *growled savagely*, but then his thought changed and he laughed. "The people were here," he said happily. "They didn't know who it was, and they were frightened. They filled up the hole the way a gopher does. This time I'll hide, and when they come to fill the hole, I'll tell them who I am. Then they will love me."

---

ghost-ridden—occupied by spirits of the dead
pick the stars with gentle fingers—he pretends to take the stars from the sky
cave in—fall
growled savagely—made angry animal sounds

65   And Tularecito dug out the hole and made it much deeper than before, because much of the dirt was loose. Just before daylight, he *retired* into the brush at the edge of the orchard and lay down to watch.

66   Bert Munroe walked out before breakfast to look at his trap again, and again he found the open hole. "The little devils!" he cried. "They're keeping it up, are they? I'll bet Manny is in it after all."

67   He studied the hole for a moment and then began to push dirt into it with the side of his foot. A savage growl spun him around. Tularecito came charging down upon him, leaping like a frog on his long legs, and swinging his shovel like a club.

68   When Jimmie Munroe came to call his father to breakfast, he found him lying on the pile of dirt. He was bleeding at the mouth and forehead. Shovelfuls of dirt came flying out of the pit.

69   Jimmie thought someone had killed his father and was getting ready to bury him. He ran home in a *frenzy of terror*, and by telephone summoned a band of neighbors.

70   Half a dozen men crept up on the pit. Tularecito struggled like a wounded lion, and held his own until they struck him on the head with his own shovel. Then they tied him up and took him in to jail.

71   In Salinas a *medical board* examined the boy. When the doctors asked him questions, he smiled *blandly* at them and did not answer. Franklin Gomez told the board what he knew and asked the *custody* of him.

72   "We really can't do it, Mr. Gomez," the judge said finally. "You say he is a good boy. Just yesterday he tried to kill a man. You must see that we cannot let him go loose. Sooner or later he will succeed in killing someone."

73   After a short *deliberation*, he committed Tularecito to the *asylum for the criminal insane* at Napa.

---

retired—went back
frenzy of terror—wild fright
medical board—group of doctors
blandly—gently; mildly
custody—care (in a legal sense)
deliberation—discussion
asylum for the criminal insane—mental hospital for dangerous people

RETELLING

Tularecito, which _____ Little _____ in

_____, is the _____ of a

_____ who was _____ in the

_____ by a _____ _____

named _____. Tularecito is a very _____

boy, with a small _____, short _____ and

_____ legs. As he _____

_____, his _____ remains

_____, although his _____ becomes very

_____, like that of a grown _____.

Tularecito _____ a lot, and he is a

_____ person. He has a _____: he can

_____ things out of _____, and he can

_____ _____ of all kinds of

_____. Tularecito's _____ are very

_____, and if people _____ anything he

has _____, he _____ very

_____ and _____ them.

When Miss Morgan _____ to _____ in

the school, she _____ about Tularecito, and she

_____ him to _____ _____ of

_____. Miss Morgan is _____ with the

other students because she _____ _____

to them every _____. Tularecito doesn't

_____ attention to these _____ until Miss

Morgan _____ to _____

_____ stories to the class. Then he _____

very _____ when she _____ about

_____.

One day, Miss Morgan _____ _____

home from school, she _____ Tularecito on a

_____ road, and she is _____, because she

doesn't _____ what Tularecito _____. He

_____ to _____ about _____.

He says that he _____ them, although he

_____ never _____ them. Miss Morgan

_____ Tularecito to _____ for

_____ at _____, because they

_____ only in the _____.

Tularecito is _____, because he _____

that he has _____ his own _____ who

_____ in the _____. At last, he is

_____ _____ to be with

_____. Tularecito _____ a deep

_____ at the _____ of a

_____ _____ in Bert Munroe's

_____. Bert Munroe _____ the

_____ and _____ it up again. He

_____ his son, Manny, about the _____,

because he _____ that Manny has _____

it.

Tularecito thinks that the _____ have

_____ the _____, because they were

_____. So Tularecito _____ a new

_____ that is _____ than the

_____ one. Then he _____ and

_____ in the brush near the _____.

When Bert Munroe _____ the new

_____, he _____ to _____ it

with _____. Tularecito _____ Bert Munroe

with a _____.

When Jimmie, Bert Munroe's _____, finds his

_____, he _____ that _____

has _____ to _____ him, and Jimmie

_____ a _____ of _____ to

_____ him. _____ men

_____ Tularecito. They _____ him with a

_____ and _____ him to

_____.

At the _____ in Salinas, a group of

_____ asks Tularecito _____, but he

_____ not _____ them. The

_____ decide that Tularecito is _____ and

that he may _____ in _____ someone.

Therefore, they _____ Tularecito to the

_____ at Napa.

STRUCTURE AND STYLE

Connections: A. Telling and Showing

"Tularecito" is a narrative, a story that John Steinbeck tells us. Its main character is Tularecito, but Miss Morgan, the teacher, is very important, too. A "character" is a particular, individual human

being, and the writer's task is to make characters we can understand and believe. To create such characters, writers work in two
basic ways: they *tell* us things about characters, and they *show* us
how characters think, feel, and act.

In "Tularecito" Steinbeck shows us his characters in action, and
he tells us about them, too. The following exercises will help you
to see how Steinbeck works.

1. Tularecito

Telling: Steinbeck tells us that Miss Morgan thinks Tularecito is a
"half-wit" and "a queer unfinished child."

Showing: Where and how does Steinbeck show us these characteristics? Find the passages in which Tularecito thinks, feels and
acts like a half-wit and a queer unfinished child.

Telling: Steinbeck tells us that Pancho is afraid of Tularecito.

Showing: Where and how does Steinbeck show us Pancho's
fear?

Telling: Steinbeck tells us that "all his life (Tularecito) had been
an alien, a lonely outcast, and now he was going home. . . ."

Showing: Where and how does Steinbeck show us Tularecito's
attempts to "go home?"

2. Miss Morgan

Telling: Steinbeck tells us that Miss Morgan "brought with her a
breathless enthusiasm for her trade. . . ."

Showing: How does Miss Morgan demonstrate her "breathless
enthusiasm?"

Telling: Miss Morgan is "vastly impressed by Tularecito."

Showing: What does she do for him?

Telling: Because of Miss Morgan's work with fairy tales, "a
change came over Tularecito."

Showing: How does Tularecito change?

B. Dialogue and Character

Steinbeck shows us the differences among his characters in the
way that they talk to themselves (what they think) or to each other
(what they say).

1. Tularecito

How does Tularecito talk to Pancho?

Is his language different when he talks to Miss Morgan? How?

Is the language Tularecito uses when he talks to himself different from the language he uses with Pancho and Miss Morgan? How?

2. Miss Morgan

How does Miss Morgan talk to Tularecito?

Is her language different when she writes a letter? How?

LAST WORDS

There is something puzzling and troubling in this story. Miss Morgan "liked to believe in whole populations who believed in fairies." She believes that "man wants most to leave some record of himself . . . on the lives of other people. . . ." When Tularecito becomes interested in gnomes, because "(he) knew about them . . .", Miss Morgan wondered if "his life (wouldn't) be richer and happier if he did believe in gnomes."

Did Miss Morgan herself really believe in gnomes? Why does she ask herself: "What harm could it possibly do" (for Tularecito to believe in them)?

Miss Morgan looks at Tularecito and thinks: "She would carve a lovely story that would be far more real than a book story ever could. . . ." What does she plan to do? Is there anything about her plan that troubles you? Why?

Finally, Miss Morgan thinks: "With a few suggestive words she had been able to make (Tularecito's) life unreal and very wonderful, and separated from the stupid lives about him. . . ." Is she correct in her belief?

Is Miss Morgan responsible for what happens to Tularecito? If she isn't, then who is?

How do you feel about Miss Morgan at the end of the story?

17
THE FILIPINO AND THE DRUNKARD

William Saroyan

HEAD NOTES

See page 49.

CULTURAL NOTES

America has been described as "a nation of nations:" a society in which people of different nationalities, colors, and beliefs have learned to live together. Generally speaking, this is true. However, there has been a long history of conflict between the majority—white Americans—and the minorities—Americans of different colors and beliefs.

This conflict—racism—is the theme of William Saroyan's story. It takes place on a ferry boat that travels across the bay from San Francisco to Oakland. The attacker is a veteran of the war in Europe. The victim is an immigrant from the Philippine Islands. The witnesses are described only as a crowd of "white people."

The story moves very swiftly; the entire action—from the opening insult to the death of the attacker—happens in perhaps ten minutes. Saroyan acts as a reporter, recording each move. He tells us and shows us only what we need to know. But he ends the story with a very difficult question, which the story reveals but does not answer.

STRATEGIES

As you read "The Filipino and the Drunkard" you should try to find *motives*: why people act in certain ways. These questions will help you:

Why does "the loud-mouthed guy" behave as he does?

Why does he refer to himself as "a real American?"

He repeats (three times) that he was "wounded twice in the war." Why is this so important to him?

Saroyan tells us that the attacker swears a lot. Why is his swearing important?

Why does the Filipino boy try to escape from his attacker?

Why does the Filipino boy's bitterness turn to rage?

Does he want to kill his attacker?

Why does he stab his attacker?

What is the crowd's reaction to the Filipino boy?

Why does he shout at the crowd?

The Filipino and the Drunkard

William Saroyan

1   This *loud-mouthed guy* in the brown camel-hair coat was not really mean, he was drunk. He took a sudden dislike to the small well-dressed Filipino and began to order him around the waiting room, telling him to get back, not to crowd up among the white people. They were waiting to get on the boat and cross the bay to Oakland. If he hadn't been drunk no one would have bothered to notice him at all, but as it was, he was making a *commotion* in the waiting room, and while everyone seemed to be in sympathy with the Filipino, no one seemed to want to *bother* about coming to the boy's *rescue*, and the poor Filipino was becoming very frightened.

2   He stood among the people, and this drunkard kept pushing up against him and saying, I told you to get back. Now get back. Go away back. I fought twenty-four months in France. I'm a real American. I don't want you standing up here among white people.

3   The boy kept squeezing *nimbly* and politely out of the drunkard's way, hurrying through the crowd, not saying anything and trying his best to be as *decent* as possible. He kept *dodging in and out*, with the drunkard stumbling after him, and as time went on the drunkard's dislike grew and he began to swear at the boy. He kept saying, "You fellows are the best-dressed men in San Francisco, and you make your money washing dishes. You've got no right to wear such fine clothes."

4   He swore a lot, and it got so bad that a lot of ladies had to imagine they were deaf and weren't hearing any of the things he was saying.

5   When the big door opened, the young Filipino moved swiftly among the people, *fleeing* from the drunkard, reaching the boat before anyone else. He ran to a corner, sat down for a moment, then got up and began looking for a more hidden place. At the other end of the boat was the drunkard. He could hear the man swearing. He looked about for a place to hide, and

---

loud-mouthed guy—someone who talks too much and too loudly
commotion—disturbance
bother—here, care
rescue—help
nimbly—quickly
decent—polite
dodging in and out—moving through the crowd
fleeing—running away

rushed into the *lavatory*. He went into one of the open *compartments* and *bolted* the door.

6   The drunkard entered the lavatory and began asking others in the room if they had seen the boy. He was a real American, he said. He had been wounded twice in the War.

7   In the lavatory he swore more freely, using words he could never use where women were present. He began to stoop and look beyond the shut doors of the various compartments. I beg your pardon, he said to those he was not seeking, and when he came to the compartment where the boy was standing, he began swearing and demanding that the boy come out.

8   "You can't get away from me," he said. "You got no right to use a place white men use. Come out or I'll break the door."

9   "Go away," the boy said.

10   The drunkard began to pound the door.

11   "You got to come out sometime," he said. "I'll wait here till you do."

12   "Go away," said the boy. "I've done nothing to you."

13   He wondered why none of the men in the lavatory had the *decency* to calm the drunkard and take him away, and then he realized there were no other men in the lavatory.

14   "Go away," he said.

15   The drunkard answered with curses, pounding the door.

16   Behind the door, the boy's bitterness grew to rage. He began to tremble, not fearing the man but fearing the rage growing in himself. He brought the knife from his pocket and drew open the sharp blade, holding the knife in his fist so tightly that the nails of his fingers cut into the flesh of his palm.

17   "Go away," he said. "I have a knife. I do not want any trouble."

18   The drunkard said he was an American. Twenty-four months in France. Wounded twice. Once in the leg, and once in the thigh. He would not go

---

lavatory—wash-room and toilet
compartments—toilet stalls
bolted—locked
decency—good and appropriate judgment

away. He was afraid of no dirty little *yellow-belly* Filipino with a knife. Let the Filipino come out, he was an American.

19   "I will kill you," said the boy. "I do not want to kill any man. You are drunk. Go away."

20   "Please do not make any trouble," he said earnestly.

21   He could hear the motor of the boat pounding. It was like his rage pounding. It was a feeling of having been humiliated, chased about and made to hide, and now it was a wish to be free, even if he had to kill. He threw the door open and tried to rush beyond the man, the knife tight in his fist, but the drunkard caught him by the sleeve and drew him back. The sleeve of the boy's coat ripped, and the boy turned and thrust the knife into the side of the drunkard, feeling it scrape against rib-bone. The drunkard shouted and screamed at once, then caught the boy at the throat, and the boy began to thrust the knife into the side of the man many times, as a boxer *jabs in the clinches*.

22   When the drunkard could no longer hold him and had fallen to the floor, the boy rushed from the room, the knife still in his hand, blood dripping from the blade, his hat gone, his hair *mussed*, and the sleeve of his coat badly torn.

23   Everyone knew what he had done, yet no one moved.

24   The boy ran to the front of the boat, seeking some place to go, then ran back to a corner, no one daring to speak to him, and everyone *aware* of his crime.

25   There was no place to go, and before the officers of the boat arrived he stopped suddenly and began to shout at the people.

26   "I did not want to hurt him," he said. "Why didn't you stop him? Is it right to chase a man like a rat? You knew he was drunk. I did not want to hurt him, but he would not let me go. He tore my coat and tried to choke me. I told him I would kill him if he would not go away. It is not my fault. I must go to Oakland to see my brother. He is sick. Do you think I am looking for trouble when my brother is sick? Why didn't you stop him?"

---

yellow-belly — cowardly
jabs in the clinches — strikes his opponent whom he is holding close
mussed — messy; untidy
aware — knowing

RETELLING

There are two ways to interpret the events in Saroyan's story. The first interpretation follows from Saroyan's opening line. The second interpretation is quite different. Examine both interpretations and choose the one that you think is closest to the truth. If you think a third interpretation is possible, write your own.

A. As Saroyan tells us at the _____ of the

_____, the _____ "wasn't really

_____, he was _____." He

_____ the young _____ for that

_____. The _____ didn't really

_____ to _____ the Filipino. He

_____ the Filipino and _____ at him.

Maybe the drunkard _____ the Filipino, too. He told

the Filipino that he was _____ _____, but

he was only a _____ _____.

The _____ was a _____ in the war,

and he was _____. He is a _____ man

and a _____ but nobody _____ about

him. He is a _____, and he is _____. He

wanted to _____ the Filipino, but he

_____ _____ to _____ him.

The Filipino got _____ and _____

away from the _____. The _____

thought the _____ was _____ and

_____ him. The Filipino moved _____

and _____ to _____ the "drunkard." This

was _____. He _____ have

_____ in the _____.

He _____ _____ gotten _____

from someone. He never _____ for

_____. But he _____ the

_____ instead, and then he _____ at the

_____ because they _____

_____ anything.

   B. Saroyan _____ us that the "loud-mouthed

_____ wasn't really _____, he was

_____." After _____ the story, I

_____ that Saroyan's "drunkard" _____

the _____ because he wasn't _____. The

"drunkard" was really a _____. When he was

_____ he _____ able to

_____ his true _____.

   The "drunkard" was _____ _____ a

_____. He _____ the Filipino and

_____ at him. The "drunkard" wanted to

_____ the Filipino _____. The Filipino

_____ _____ and _____ in

the lavatory because he was _____.

   Why did the "drunkard" _____ the Filipino?

Because he _____ to _____ him. Why

did the "drunkard" _____ at the Filipino? Because

he _____ to _____ him.

_____ the _____ successful?

   If the _____ had done _____, the

"drunkard" would _____ been _____.

But the Filipino _____ angry, and his

_____ grew to _____. If the "drunkard"

hadn't _____ to _____ the Filipino from

_____ _____, nothing _____

_____ happened. But the "drunkard"

_____ a _____, and the Filipino

_____ him. He _____ _____

to _____ the "drunkard" but he _____

no other _____. The _____ wouldn't

_____ him.

STRUCTURE AND STYLE

Connections: Verb + *-ing*

Compare these two pairs of structures.

   They *were waiting* to get on the boat . . .

   He *was making* a commotion . . .

   The boy kept squeezing . . . *hurrying* through the crowd, not *saying* anything . . .

   The young Filipino moved swiftly . . . *fleeing* from the people, *reaching* the boat . . .

   Notice that the italicized forms of the verb look alike. They all end in *-ing*. But they are used differently. The verb + *-ing* in the first pair are finite verb phrases. The verb + *-ing* in the second pair are nonfinite verb phrases, and they are used as modifiers: like adjectives modifying *the boy* and *the young Filipino*.

These nonfinite verb phrases in the second pair do not have tense, like the verb phrases in the first pair (past continuous). Their lack of tense allows them to modify noun phrases.

Nonfinite verb phrases may come before or after the noun phrase they modify:

He walked a little further.

He saw the river clearly then.

Walking a little further, he . . . (before)

He walked a little further, seeing . . . (after)

A writer uses nonfinite verb phrases for at least two reasons: to make the prose move more rapidly; instead of periods (stops), the phrases use commas (pauses) and keep moving; and to say more with fewer words:

He could hear the man.

The man was swearing.

He could hear the man swearing.

1. To see how Saroyan uses nonfinite verb phrases in "The Filipino and the Drunkard," underline all the examples that you find. (Note: *keep* + verb + *-ing* and *begin* + verb + *-ing* are finite verb phrases. Don't underline these structures.)

How important is the nonfinite verb phrase in Saroyan's style?

2. The following narrative can be improved if you use nonfinite verb phrases carefully. Study the narrative and decide which sentences you will change. Then rewrite the narrative, making the changes.

David unlocked the door and entered the house. He turned on the light in the hallway. He called his wife's name. There was no answer. He sighed and realized that his wife was late again.

David put down his briefcase. He removed his jacket and hung it over a chair. He walked into the kitchen. He opened the door of the refrigerator. He examined the food on the shelves. David spoke out loud. He said, "Someone forgot to buy food for dinner." David removed the ice-tray from the freezer. He said, "I guess I'll have a drink instead."

David poured some whiskey into a glass and added ice and water. The telephone rang. David held his drink in one hand and answered the telephone. He spoke softly and said "Hello." His wife said, "Hello, David. Are you starving?"

David sipped his drink and answered, "Yes. No one did any shopping."

His wife laughed. She said, "Let me take you out for dinner. I've just gotten a big raise. Can you meet me at Restaurant Michel in twenty minutes?" she asked.

David smiled. He answered, "I never pass up an opportunity. You know that."

How many nonfinite phrases did you use?

Have you improved the style of the narrative? How?

LAST WORDS

At three points in the story, Saroyan refers to members of the crowd watching the drunkard and the Filipino.

". . . while everyone seemed to be in sympathy with the Filipino, no one seemed to want to bother about coming to the boy's rescue . . ." (beginning)

"He wondered why none of the men in the lavatory had the decency to calm the drunkard and take him away . . ." (middle)

"I did not want to hurt him . . . why didn't you stop him? . . . It is not my fault . . . why didn't you stop him?" (end)

Who is responsible for the violence that occurs? No one in the crowd does anything. Is the observer of a violent act innocent because he or she does nothing? The attacker was drunk. Is drunkenness an excuse for violence? The Filipino seems to say to the crowd: "You made me do it." Is that an excuse for his violence?

If you had been a member of the crowd, what would you have done? When? How? Why?

V
WISDOM

18

SAM
AND THE
RUTABAGAS

Arthur Hoppe

HEAD NOTES

Arthur Hoppe (rhymes with *poppy*) is a journalist who lives and works in San Francisco. He writes a newspaper column called "Arthur Hoppe" six times a week for the San Francisco *Chronicle*. Mr. Hoppe is a writer of considerable wit and talent, who observes the foolishness, craziness, and sorrow of modern life. His work has been collected and published in two books. The two fables that you will read are from *The Perfect Solution to Absolutely Every-thing*.

CULTURAL NOTES

The setting for "Sam and the Rutabagas" is California in the troubled 1960s. During the decade from 1960 to 1970, American society was experiencing several different kinds of shocks. President John F. Kennedy was assassinated in Dallas. Later, his brother, Robert Kennedy was killed by a gunman in Los Angeles. Martin Luther King, the leader of the black and white Americans who opposed segregation, was killed in Memphis. Many women in America joined together in a feminist movement that opposed unfair treatment of women. And there was opposition to American participation in the war in Vietnam. Historians of this period refer to the "second American revolution": opposition to unfair racial and sexual policies and to the power of the "military industrial complex."

This opposition appeared in both active and passive ways. Actively, people protested against the government, institutions— like universities and businesses—and even against parents or older people. A slogan that appeared in the 1960s was "Never trust anyone over 30." Passively, some people began to "drop out"—to forget about society's problems.

Students on the campuses of American colleges and universities used both kinds of protest. There were student strikes, protest marches, and "sit-ins" (the occupation of university property by protesting students). And there were also students who "dropped out" because they opposed the policies of the government and the university. Arthur Hoppe observes both types of protest in his two fables.

STRATEGIES

When you read the title of Arthur Hoppe's book—*The Perfect Solution to Absolutely Everything*—you may wonder how serious he is. You know that there aren't many perfect solutions in the world. To "absolutely everything?" No. Impossible. Why would a writer use a title like that?

Arthur Hoppe is a serious writer. He usually writes satire, a form of prose that makes fun of serious problems, foolish practices, and foolish people. In "Sam and the Rutabagas," Mr. Hoppe's theme is the conflict between freedom and authority, a serious and complicated problem. But he writes about it simply and humorously. Let these questions guide you as you read this fable:

"Sam and the Rutabagas" begins with "Once upon a time . . . ." What kinds of writing usually begin this way?

How does Sam first experience authority?

How does Sam first experience freedom from authority?

What does Sam learn at the university?

How does Sam use his freedom at the university?

How are Sam's father and the university authorities alike?

How does Sam become like his father?

How is Sam Junior like Sam?

Sam and the Rutabagas

Arthur Hoppe

1   Once upon a time there was a little boy named Sam. He was a good little boy and did almost everything his father told him to do. When his father said, "Brush your teeth," he brushed his teeth. When his father said, "Eat your rutabaga," he ate his rutabaga. And so forth. Each time he did what his father said, his father was very, very happy. As for Sam, he liked making his father happy. But he never did learn to care much for *rutabaga*.

2   Of course, like most little boys, Sam sometimes didn't do what he was told. Once he chewed gum in school. Once he went swimming in the abandoned *quarry*. And once he rode his bicycle in the street. All of which he enjoyed much more than eating rutabaga. Each time Sam's father heard of such *transgressions*, he would look up from his bills and say, "Dammit, you must learn more respect for authority." When Sam asked why, his father would snap, "Because I say so." Or, "Shut up and eat your rutabaga."

3   Determined to learn why he should respect authority, Sam went to the greatest university in the whole wide world. It had lots and lots of authority. The Regents, the President, the Chancellor and all the Deans were for authority. The faculty wrote long *dissertations* on "The Role of Authority in a Free Society," a problem they examined *minutely* from every *conceivable angle*. But the students, of course, were against authority. They were for freedom.

4   "Freedom," cried Sam, "is much better than authority!" He joined the Free Speech Movement, the Free Sex League, and *cadged* free lunches whenever possible. He wrote *free verse*, practiced *free love*, and passed out *anarchist pamphlets* in his free time. He grew a beard because the authorities didn't like beards, and wore sandals because the authorities didn't like

---

rutabaga—a large, yellowish root vegetable; a turnip
quarry—a place where stone is dug for building
transgressions—bad deeds; breaking rules
dissertations—scholarly studies
minutely—very carefully
conceivable angle—possible point of view
cadged—begged
free verse—unrhymed poetry
free love—sex without marriage
anarchist pamphlets—statements against organized government

sandals. Sometimes he didn't brush his teeth for *two days running* and he *swore* never, never to eat another rutabaga as long as he lived.

5   He was very, very happy.

6   The authorities, of course, said, "Dammit, you must learn more respect for authority." But Sam didn't care because he was happy and he liked freedom better. And his girl friend, Nellie Jo, agreed. They agreed on everything. In fact, when Sam graduated, they agreed to get married. Sam got a job to support them and bought a house for them to live in and an electric toothbrush to brush their teeth with. In time, Sam Junior *came along*. But he was a good little boy and did almost everything his father told him to do. Which made his father very, very happy. Of course, sometimes Sam Junior didn't do what he was told. When this happened Sam would look up from his bills and say, "Dammit, you've got to learn more respect for authority."

7   Moral: This is truly the best of all possible worlds. The young like freedom and the old like authority. Thus each of us is happy with what he's got.

RETELLING

This time, you are going to write a short composition about your own experiences with authority and freedom. It will contain three paragraphs. The opening (topic) sentence of each paragraph will be given. Then there will be some questions for you to answer in sentences of your own.

Paragraph 1

I first learned about authority from my _____ when

I was _____(age)_____.

Where were you?

What happened?

How did you feel about the experience?

---

two days running—two days in a row
swore—promised faithfully
came along—was born

Paragraph 2

I had my first taste of freedom when _____ .

Where were you?

What happened?

How did you feel about the experience?

Paragraph 3

Now that I'm an adult, I realize that both authority and freedom are necessary.

What kinds of authority are necessary?

What kinds of freedom are necessary?

When do they conflict with each other?

What do you do about the conflict?

STRUCTURE AND STYLE

Connections: A. Repetitions of Words and Phrases

In "Sam and the Rutabagas," Arthur Hoppe repeats certain words or phrases several times. To see how often these repetitions happen, read through "Sam and the Rutabagas" again and underline these words or phrases as they occur in various parts of the narrative.

once	sometimes
each time	but
very, very happy	almost everything
of course	

We can divide the narrative into three parts: (1) Sam as a child; (2) Sam as a student; (3) Sam as a father. Which of the words and phrases occur in parts 1 & 2? Which ones occur in all three parts?

Why do you think the writer repeats these words and phrases?

B. Repetitions of Sentences

The following sentences are repeated in exactly the same way or in a similar way:

"He was a good little boy and did almost everything his father told him to do."

"Of course, like most little boys, Sam sometimes didn't do what he was told."

"Each time Sam's father heard of such transgressions, he would look up from his bills and say, 'Dammit, you must learn more respect for authority.' "

In which parts of the narrative do these repetitions occur?

Why do you think the writer repeats these sentences?

LAST WORDS

A fable is a short narrative, a little story, that tries to teach us something important about our lives. Fables contain a *moral*: a truth, a "moral teaching" of some kind.

Examine Arthur Hoppe's moral.

Is he serious when he tells us "This is truly the best of all possible worlds?"

His reason for saying this is "the young like freedom and the old like authority." Do you believe that this is a true statement? What are your reasons?

"Thus each of us is happy with what he's got." Does he mean that the young don't need and don't have authority? Does he mean that the old don't need and don't have freedom? How could either group be happy in these conditions?

19
THE PERFECT PILL

Arthur Hoppe

HEAD NOTES

See page 177.

CULTURAL NOTES

See page 177.

STRATEGIES

In "The Perfect Pill," Arthur Hoppe has invented a young man whom he calls Aristotle Spinoza. The two names come from famous philosophers: Aristotle, the Greek philosopher of the fourth century B.C., and Baruch Spinoza, the Dutch philosopher of the seventeenth century A.D.

Let these questions guide you as you read the narrative:

Why would Hoppe use such famous names for an ordinary young man?

Why would anyone "drop out" if he "wanted to save the human race?"

How does LSD improve matters?

Why isn't LSD a perfect solution?

Why was Aristotle's Perfect Pill so successful?

Why did the Perfect Pill finally fail?

What is a sloth? What are its characteristics?

The Perfect Pill

Arthur Hoppe

1   Once upon a time there was a young man named Aristotle Spinoza who wanted to save the human race. So he *dropped out*.

---

dropped out—refused to do what others do

2   "Cleanliness is *overrated*," said Aristotle to himself. "*Social taboos* against long hair are silly. It's hate, greed and *striving* that ruin the world. The human race will never be saved until we all come to love each other."

3   So he gave up baths, grew his hair long and went to live in a *hippie pad*. Right away, Aristotle ran into several minor problems and one major one. The minor ones included *underarm offensiveness*, an itchy neck and chronic indigestion. The major one was that, try as he might, he couldn't bring himself to love everybody—particularly one bearded roommate given to playing the *sitar* at 2 A.M. and eating crackers in bed.

4   Aristotle took his problems to a *guru*. "Hmmm," said the guru, "how many *micrograms* of acid are you taking?"

5   "Acid?" asked Aristotle.

6   "Lysergic acid. LSD. It will increase your awareness, expand your consciousness, and you will love everybody," said the guru solemnly. "Take 250 micrograms twice weekly four hours after eating. Next."

7   And it worked! After taking LSD, Aristotle saw pretty colors, heard pretty sounds, smelled pretty smells, felt pretty feelings, and loved everybody. He even *equated* the noise of crackers being *munched* in bed with Beethoven's Fifth Symphony. But these effects wore off in eight hours. And most of the time he itched, smelled, *burped* and couldn't stand sitar music.

8   "LSD is fine, but it isn't perfect," he said thoughtfully. "What the human race needs is The Perfect Pill."

9   After many an experiment, he invented it. The Perfect Pill contained an itch reliever, a *deodorant*, an antacid tablet and, unlike LSD, it *turned you on* permanently. The Perfect Pill was an instant success. Soon everybody in the world was turned on permanently. Hate, greed, striving and silly social

---

overrated—too important
social taboos—limits
striving—overwork
hippie pad—a place where other drop-outs live
underarm offensiveness—smelly armpits
sitar—a stringed instrument from India
guru—spiritual advisor (Indian religion)
micrograms—thousandths of a gram; a small amount
equated—made equal
munched—chewed
burped—belched
deodorant—a substance to stop underarm odor
turned you on—made you happy

taboos disappeared. Everybody sat around seeing pretty colors, listening to pretty sounds, smelling pretty smells, feeling pretty feelings and loving each other.

10   Of course, while no one *bothered* to go to war any more, no one bothered to build bridges, have children or explore the universe any more, either. And after a few hundred years of sitting around loving each other the human race died off. It was replaced by the three-toed *sloth*, a gentle creature. "It's *your bag* now," said the last man to the three-toed sloth. "But I notice you don't take pills. Have you found some better way to love each other?"

11   "*Naturally*," said the three-toed sloth.

12   Moral: If the only way people can be *induced* to love one another is through *ingesting* chemicals the human race deserves what it gets.

RETELLING

Once again, you will have an opportunity to write a little composition of your own. It will be in the form of a dialogue. Half of the dialogue will be given. You will write the other half. (Use a separate sheet of paper for this assignment.) The dialogue goes like this.

You believe that stupidity, ignorance, and laziness ruin the world. You invent a Perfect Pill to solve these problems. A newspaper reporter is interviewing you. The reporter asks several questions.

R: ___(your name)___ , let me ask you a few questions about your Perfect Pill. First, what is it supposed to cure?

You:

R: I see. So people who take the pill will get smarter and work harder.

---

bothered—wanted to; made the effort
sloth—a slow-moving, vegetarian animal
your bag—your turn; your problem
naturally—here, two meanings: (1) by natural means; (2) of course
induced—led; shown how
ingesting—here, eating or taking pills

You:

R: How many pills per day will people have to take?

You:

R: Okay. And how much does each pill cost?

You:

R: Which countries in the world need your pill?

You:

R: Will everyone in those countries need to take the Perfect Pill?

You:

R: What will the results be? How will the pill change the world?

You:

R: Why will smarter, hard-working people be happier?

You:

R: But _____, isn't it true that lazy, stupid people don't cause the real problems of the world—like wars and depressions?

You:

R: Yes, I see, but wouldn't the world be a better place if people moved more slowly and were kind to each other?

You:

R: Okay. Well, what are you going to do with all the money you make from the Perfect Pill?

You:

STRUCTURE AND STYLE

Connections: Series

In "The Perfect Pill," Arthur Hoppe uses groups of words and clauses (sentences) in a series: words and sentences that follow each other. His series join three to five words or sentences. Here are two examples.

"It's *hate*, *greed*, and *striving* that ruin the world." (words)

"So *he gave up baths*, *grew his hair long*, and *went to live in a hippie pad*." (clauses)

Read "The Perfect Pill" again and underline all the series that Hoppe uses.

How important is the use of the series in Hoppe's style?

Choose one sentence using a series and try to rewrite it *without* using a series. What happens? How would Hoppe's style change, as a result?

LAST WORDS

At the end of "The Perfect Pill," the sloth says, "Naturally." This word can have two meanings here. What are they? Are both meanings possible here? Does Hoppe want to confuse us or make us laugh?

Consider the moral at the end of the fable. Does Hoppe seem to criticize the use of "chemicals" to make people love each other? What makes you think so?

20
A MISER

W. S. Merwin

HEAD NOTES

As a young child, William Merwin (1927–) wrote religious songs for his father who was a minister in New Jersey. He has been writing ever since in both English and Spanish, and he has won many prizes. Merwin uses forms from other cultures and other traditions including the Greeks and the Bible. He has translated many works into Spanish. Cervantes, the seventeenth-century Spanish novelist, is one of his favorite writers. Merwin is very concerned about ecology, the condition of the earth, and his poetry speaks with a hopeful voice about man's destructive activities in the natural world. He is also a novelist.

CULTURAL NOTES

Usually, a poem or a prose piece comes from a cultural setting: a place and a time that are real or imaginary. In Merwin's little story, "A Miser," we have neither a place nor a time. Their absence gives Merwin freedom to tell his story without reference to anything or anyone that requires description or explanation. The story that Merwin presents is a philosophical problem.

Like Arthur Hoppe, Merwin is sometimes a writer of satire. One question he presents in "A Miser" is this: If someone takes something valuable from our world, and we don't even notice its absence, then what kind of people are we? Merwin also presents a second question: If only one person can take away a value from the world, how many people will be necessary to restore this value to the world?

STRATEGIES

You may know the story of King Midas, the most famous miser in literature. Because everything that Midas touched turned to gold, he was in danger of starving to death. There is a similar problem in Merwin's story.

Let these questions guide you as you read it.

We don't know why the miser took laughter from the world. We do know that his plan was a failure. How do we know this?

The miser wants people to know what laughter was like. Why? What does he tell people about laughter?

After many efforts to interest other people in laughter, the miser has no success. Why?

The miser's luck changes when "somebody else laughed." What is the danger here?

Does the miser finally succeed or fail in keeping all the laughter in the world? Why?

A Miser

W. S. Merwin

1   A man was able to *get hold of* all the laughter in the world, and he packed it tightly and locked it up in his house and hid the key.

2   The trouble was that nobody missed it.

3   He had to tell them what they were *missing*. Nobody knew what he was talking about. Nobody believed him. Nobody thought that what he was talking about was real. Who could believe that, after all? Would anyone believe it if someone came up and said that they had all the laughter in the world locked up somewhere? Would anyone believe it, even if neither of them laughed?

4   He tried to describe laughter to them. He showed them how it was done. He showed different ways in which different people could laugh. He told them all the things that made people do it, everything he could remember or invent. People falling down. *Filth*. People making terrible mistakes. People unable to control themselves. *Misfortunes* of all kinds. People with something the matter with them. No interest.

5   He told them that it would be good for their health, and that he would not make it expensive for them. No interest.

6   There were many things about it that he didn't even know, he said. No interest.

7   It had been called *divine*, he said. No interest.

---

get hold of — take
missing — lacking; didn't have
filth — anything dirty
misfortunes — accidents; bad luck
divine — heavenly; god-like

8 But the man kept on trying. Because at least at night he could always go home and take out the key and open up *some* and have a good laugh to himself. But then one night he started to laugh at himself, and that made him lonely.

9 He tried to invite somebody else in to laugh. But it was very hard. He even said he would give the laughter away.

10 At that somebody else laughed.

11 So that person remembered how to laugh. So that person was *on his side*. They were laughing together. Somebody else was laughing with him.

12 But that meant that somebody else had some of the laughter in the world. So he started making plans to steal it.

13 But the other kept giving it away.

RETELLING

Merwin's story grows out of two common verbs: *take* ("got hold of") and *give* ("away"). A great deal of the world's activity depends on these two verbs. Misers try to take and keep everything. Spendthrifts try to give everything away. Most of us live somewhere between these two extremes.

Let's use Merwin's story as a model for a miser or a spend-thrift. You may choose to write *either* of the following two stories.

"A Miser"

"Once there was a miser who got hold of all the freedom in a country. He put it in a prison and locked the door. He put the key in his pocket and waited."

Continue the story, answering these questions as you go.

Did anyone notice that freedom was gone?

How did people live their lives?

Did anyone want freedom again? What did he/they do?

---

some — some laughter
on his side — like him

Did people take their freedom from the miser? How did they do this?

What happened to the miser?

What did people learn from this experience?

"A Spendthrift"

"Once there was a spendthrift. He believed that everyone and everything in his country should be free. He got hold of thousands of keys, and he unlocked the doors of prisons, mental hospitals, and zoos. He freed all the people and the animals. Then he waited to see what would happen."

Continue the story, answering these questions as you go.

Did people notice any difference in society?

How did people live their lives?

Did anyone want to change things? What did he/they want to do?

Did people try to take the keys from the spendthrift? How did they do this? What happened to the freed people and animals?

What happened to the spendthrift?

What did people learn from this experience?

STRUCTURE AND STYLE

Connections: A. Antecedents and Their Replacements

Antecedents are words that "come before" the words that replace them. Antecedents are usually nouns; but sometimes antecedents may be an entire clause: a sentence or an entire predicate (verb + noun phrase + modifiers).

Merwin's style makes use of antecedents and their replacements: words like *it* and *that*. Here are two examples:

"A man was able to get hold of all the laughter in the world, and he packed it tightly and locked it up in his house and hid the key."

"The trouble was that nobody missed *it*."

What is the antecedent for *it* in the first sentence? Is *laughter* or *key* the antecedent for *it* in the second sentence?

"Nobody thought what he was talking about was real. Who could believe *that*, after all?"

What is the antecedent for *that*?

To follow what Merwin is saying, you must understand the relationship of antecedents and their replacements. Reread "A Miser" and underline the antecedents and their replacements, usually *it* and *that*, but sometimes other words, as well.

How important is the antecedent-replacement relationship in "A Miser?"

B. *That* Clauses

Merwin uses the connective (subordinate conjunction) *that* to introduce clauses (sentences). *That* clauses function as nouns and adjectives. Here are two examples:

"The trouble was (that nobody missed it.") Function: noun

"He told them all the things (that made people do it . . . ") Function: adjective

Reread "A Miser" and enclose all the *that* clauses in parentheses. If you can decide how they are used, write noun or adjective next to the clause.

How important are *that* clauses in "A Miser?"

LAST WORDS

W. S. Merwin is making a satirical statement about what is wrong with the world. When laughter disappears from the world, "nobody missed it." What do you think that Merwin is saying about the condition of human life?

At the end of his fable, Merwin tells us "But the other kept giving it away."

Is laughter a "thing" like money or clothes?

Can laughter be bought and sold? (Think of comedy shows on television.)

How can you give laughter away?

Is there hope for human beings if one person learns to laugh and "gives (laughter) away?" Why do you or do you not think so?

21
THE
INHERITANCE

W. S. Merwin

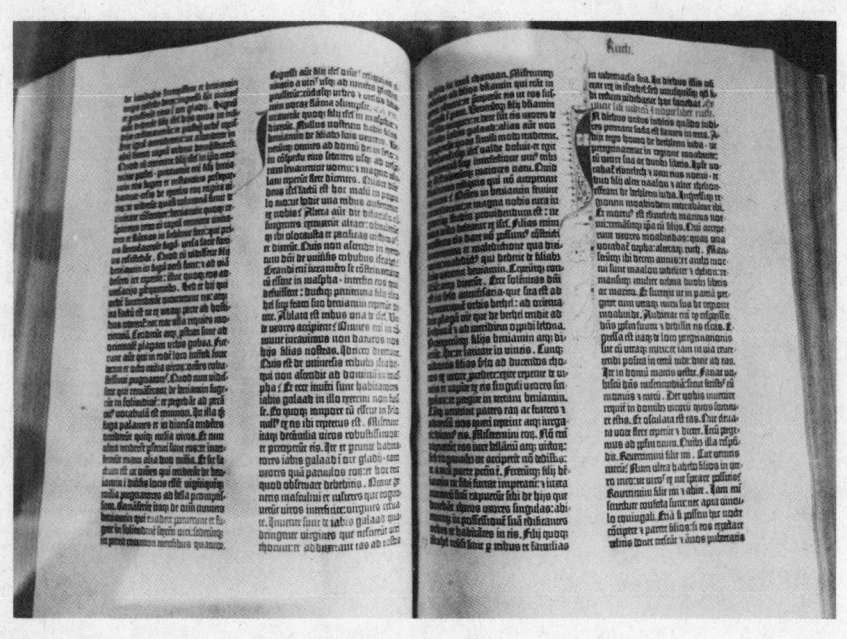

HEAD NOTES

See page 191.

CULTURAL NOTES

"The Inheritance" is like "A Miser" in several ways. First, we don't know where we are in space (place) or time (century). Second, Merwin is writing about the loss of something valuable: laughter in "A Miser" and literacy in "The Inheritance." Third, someone remembers what has been lost: "somebody" remembered how to laugh in "A Miser;" the old king "had heard of writing" in "The Inheritance."

The society that Merwin presents in "The Inheritance" is "primitive." He takes us "backward" in time. A book, a common object in our world, is puzzling and strange in this primitive society. We may wonder what has happened to the world that we know. Merwin doesn't tell us.

Merwin presents a "backward" world—one in which literacy (writing and reading symbols on a page) has been lost. People who speak different languages cannot understand each other, and there is no "universal" written language, like Latin in the Middle Ages or English today, to help them. Writing is a record of human experience. Without reading, there is no knowledge of the world beyond the individual's daily experience. Our world of science, history, philosophy, and literature is unknown to the people in Merwin's "The Inheritance."

STRATEGIES

An inheritance is something that is passed on from one person to another. We may inherit money (or debts); we can inherit physical characteristics from our parents; and we can inherit experience and knowledge from people who lived in other times and places.

The first part of "The Inheritance" puts us inside the life of a lonely, frightened shepherd. He discovers a "book" (for which he has no word in his language because he cannot read or write.) The book is the shepherd's inheritance. It is a great mystery and problem for him.

The book becomes a danger to the shepherd when Merwin says: "After that his life changed." The rest of "The Inheritance" tells us what happened to the shepherd because he tried to become literate.

Let these questions guide you as you read "The Inheritance:"

What are the tests that the shepherd uses as he tries to understand the "book?"

What do these tests tell you about the shepherd's world?

Among the objects that the shepherd "knows" are doors, tracks, and boxes. Is a book like any of these things? How?

The shepherd depends on his senses (sight, hearing, touch, etc.) to understand the world around him. How would you explain the following?

His fear of bringing his sheep into the cave "with the book there?" His description of night, stars, and wind? His experience with the wolf?

Why do you think that the shepherd's cheeks "were wet with tears?"

What is Merwin telling us in these lines?

When he touched the printed page the shepherd felt "a small lightning run up his arm."

Whenever he called the dog "he felt the tracks stir in the fingertips of his left hand."

Why does the dog seem to fear him?

What is the shepherd's method for learning to read?

The shepherd is looking for a "secret" in the book. What do you think the secret is?

After the other shepherds steal his book, the shepherd escapes. He nearly dies, but an old man saves him. Why do these terrible things happen to the shepherd? Why is he saved?

In the end, an old king in an old ruin gives the shepherd a new life and a place of respect. What does the old king want to know? Why isn't the shepherd able to teach others what he remembers from the "book?"

The Inheritance

W. S. Merwin

1   On a mountain whose name had been forgotten, a shepherd found a book in a cave.

2   He had been gathering stones to make a wall across the cave *mouth*, where he found it. It was under the last stone of a pile in a corner of the cave. He had never seen a book before. He had never heard of such a thing. He was frightened and crept back a few steps toward the cave mouth, watching it.

3   He wanted to see whether it breathed. Whether it was a thing that breathed, and if it was, he wanted to see how long it *could go* without breathing. The first and second things he wanted to know.

4   He wanted to see whether it was really dead, or only pretending to be dead. He had seen animals pretending to be dead, looking like that but shaped differently, crouched together or coiled up underneath. He had seen men pretending to be dead, looking like that but shaped differently, lying there with weapons hidden under them. He had seen, worst of all, beings that looked like men, and even looked as though they were breathing, suddenly turn into stones or logs or shadows, and pretend to be dead, only to follow him later until he was unable to tell whether he was asleep or awake. But they too were shaped differently, like logs, or stones, or shadows. Even if it was alive, this was none of those things. It must be something else. So he wanted to see what it was.

5   Then he wanted to see whether it was a door. He had heard of doors, like doors into real houses, but doors into the floors of caves. This, if it was a door, was a door like an old lost *garment* of something, gone stiff now, and strange to everyone, smelling of unending darkness, and hostile to the *infant present*. It had been lying alone in the darkness too long, the only book.

6   If it was a door it was a door like food, lying in front of him, *submissive but alien*. It had a few rows of patterns pressed into it. Tracks.

---

mouth – opening
could go – remain; survive
garment – a piece of clothing
infant present – the present moment
submissive but alien – quiet but strange

7   He bent forward and put his ear to it and listened.

8   Things might be asleep in those tracks now. Those might be their beds. The things might be out now, hunting, and come back to their beds, and he would be there. There would be many of them. He had heard of them, small people.

9   Maybe not, though.

10   He had heard of boxes. He began to want to know whether the thing was a box. He had even seen boxes. He had heard that some of the boxes still in the world had been found in dark hiding-places, in caves. Some of them had had valuable things in them, and some had had terrible things in them, and death itself hiding under the lids. Against these last, he knew, no human weapons gave protection. But he pulled his *staff* closer. The sun was going down. There was no fire.

11   It was almost dark. He afraid to touch the thing now with his hand. He was afraid to touch it just before night. But he was afraid to leave it. But he wanted to send the dog to bring the sheep up to the cave. But he couldn't bring the sheep into the cave now, with the book there. But already he could hardly see it. But when he moved forward, his own shadow, which for some time had been nothing but a shapeless cloud of darkness, moved forward also and covered the book. But he heard the sheep *rustling* and coughing outside the cave, lambs crying, not near enough. But he listened for the dog. But he could not hear it. But he thought of the night coming. Outside, in that part of his mind, stars were walking forward toward night until their lights were visible, and they came on walking, and stopped in their places, and then night carried them toward the mountains.

12   He listened for the fox.

13   He listened for the wolf.

14   He heard the wind that came after sundown and then went away by itself.

15   Then he wanted to hear whether he heard breathing in the cave, that wasn't his own breathing.

16   But then it seemed to have stopped.

17   He was listening. He was watching the place where he had last seen the thing, trying to remember exactly what it looked like.

---

staff — wooden stick
rustling — moving through the grass

18   But he kept thinking of wolves. There was one wolf he had seen many times, and he wanted to know whether it was the same wolf every time. Wherever he was, it always came alone, just at evening. He had never seen it come. Each time he had looked up and it was there, watching somewhere to one side of him. Each time he had fixed his eyes on the wolf, kept them there, almost stopped breathing, only to see, some time later, that he was watching a wolf-shaped *patch* of darkness, from which the animal had gone. He thought now that he must still be watching the wolf.

19   When the first light came into the cave he could see nothing at all in front of him. Then he felt his cheeks. They were wet with tears. Then he saw the book, and without waiting he crossed the cave, and bent down, and touched the book, and made his hand stay there. He felt a small animal, a small *lightning*, run up his arm, but it was not painful. He moved his fingers over the tracks. Then he straightened and put the fingers of his left hand into the palm of his right hand, and folded the fingers of his right hand over them, to comfort them, to talk with them and ask them. With one hand in the other, that way, he went out of the cave and down the slope.

20   The sheep were scattered. When he called the dog, he felt the tracks stir in the fingertips of his left hand. They stirred every time he called the dog. When the dog came it seemed to be afraid of him.

21   When he had the sheep together again, and the dog watching them, up by the cave, he went in to the book, and with both hands lifted an edge. When the book fell open, he knelt to look at the tracks. Many animals seemed to have passed there and he did not know any of them. When he tried to lift again, pages turned and the tracks went on. He came to the empty pages at the end. He knocked to see whether the bottom page was *hollow*. He lifted it and the whole book came up and he carried it out into the sunlight.

22   After that his life changed.

23   He stared at the book for hours every day. He wrapped it carefully in his sack when he changed *pastures*. He began to be able to remember some of the tracks. He thought there was a secret in them that he would discover. He looked for them in the world and sometimes he saw them, but alone, or in a different order, so that he thought the others must have disappeared. He began to remember the order in which the tracks came on the pages,

---

patch — a small area
lightning — electricity
hollow — empty
pastures — grassy feeding places

and some of their repetitions, some of the groups in which they travelled together, some of the companies in which some of the groups travelled.

24   He thought he was coming closer all the time to learning the secret in the book which was making the book change his life.

25   But the book had *infected him with a new fear*—of losing it. He guarded it carefully. He *avoided* other shepherds. They *became suspicious of him.* They *spied on him.* They followed him. They saw the book. They saw him open it, stare at it, kneel, staring at it. They stole it from him. They killed his dog so that he would not be able to follow them. They tried to kill him. He got away at night. He went on until nobody knew his language. He was beaten. Everything else was taken away from him. He was found in a marketplace, *begging*. As he sat there he tried to *trace* some of the lost tracks in the dust, to remember them. He was seized. He was taken away and *tortured*, while they kept asking him questions he did not understand. The tortures were stopped and an old man led him away to a tent and gave him food and had him washed and dressed in clean clothes. The next morning they set out, and he with them. They travelled for days, into the mountains. Everything got older. They came to ancient rocks, ancient trees, a huge *ruin*. A man even older than the first one seemed to be the king there.

26   They led him to understand, with gestures, that they wanted him to trace the track, in the dust. The old king came to watch him make the marks, and stared at them, and asked the shepherd questions no word of which the shepherd understood.

27   They tried to teach him their language so that he could explain what the tracks meant, because the old king had heard of writing. They tried to learn the shepherd's language, in case the meaning of the tracks could be *expressed* only in his native tongue. They learned to trace the tracks themselves, to be ready for the day when he would be able to tell their meaning.

---

infected him with a new fear—given him a new fear, like a disease
avoided—stayed away from
became suspicious of him—didn't trust him
spied on him—watched him secretly
begging—asking for food or money
trace—draw
tortured—made to suffer great pain
ruin (noun)—the remains of something destroyed
expressed—spoken; explained

28   He showed them the tracks again, here and there and in the world, and
he saw that they treated each other, afterwards, with care and *reverence*.
He never came to understand their language, nor they his, but they listened
to him, they bowed to him, they followed him, they waited on him, they
gave him a place next to the king, nodding to him as though he were *a
mute*. And to please them he went on trying to remember more tracks, till
the end of his days, *forgetting even so*, getting the order wrong, forgetting
more and more, and supplying it as best he could, *from mere habit*.

29   But he never tried to tell them where the cave was. No one ever knew.
No one even knew what mountain it was on.

RETELLING

"The Inheritance" provides an interesting model for other stories. Here is the first part of a story for you to complete using the
questions at the end.

When Mary finished shopping in the city, she got on the bus that
would take her home. Mary was carrying a large shopping bag.
There were no seats on the bus, so she put the shopping bag on
the floor and stood next to it. Thirty minutes later, she got off the
bus and walked two blocks to her house.

As she removed her purchases from the shopping bag, she
noticed something strange. There was a tiny package wrapped in
red paper. She didn't remember buying anything like that. She
opened the package. In it were three white objects. They looked
like perfect little eggs. She wondered where they had come from.
She decided to keep them and show them to her husband.

When Joseph, Mary's husband, came home from work, she
told him about the three white objects. He examined them. He
thought that they might be seeds of some kind. He took them into
the garden behind the house. He dug a hole and planted them.
Then he and Mary forgot about them.

A week later, Mary noticed a small green plant growing where
Joseph had planted the seeds. She watered it and told Joseph
about it. Joseph examined it. He thought it might be a tree of some
kind. But he had planted three seeds, and there was only one plant.
That puzzled Joseph and Mary.

---

reverence — great respect
a mute — a person unable to speak
fogetting even so — forgetting as he tried to remember
from mere habit — only from practice

After a month had passed, a small tree was growing up in the backyard. Neither Mary nor Joseph had seen anything like this tree. It grew very rapidly—almost half a meter each week. Its leaves were long and slender, like green fingers, and they trembled in the breeze.

When the tree was four meters high and still growing taller, Joseph told Mary that it was too large. He wanted to cut it down. She wanted to wait. Maybe the tree would bloom, she told Joseph. He examined the tree. Mary was right. It had hundreds of little buds on its branches.

The flowers were red and white, and they smelled wonderful. The tree attracted thousands of bees. Joseph hated bees; he was afraid of them. Mary liked bees; they never bothered her.

When the fruit came, it was shaped like the seeds, and it was red and white, like the flowers. Joseph didn't want to eat the fruit. He thought it might be poisonous. Strange seeds make strange fruit, he told Mary.

But Mary was curious, and one morning she picked some of the strange fruit. She cut one open. There was no seed inside it. She offered some sliced fruit to Joseph. At first, he refused to eat it. So Mary tried some, and Joseph watched her. She smiled and ate some more. Then Joseph took a slice and tried it. He smiled at Mary and ate all of the fruit in his bowl. They smiled and laughed.

Mary returned to the tree and brought in a basket of fruit. She and Joseph ate all of it. They laughed a lot and hugged and kissed each other. Joseph decided not to go to work that day. Later that morning, Joseph noticed that Mary was staring at him.

"Why are you staring at me?" he asked.

"You look—different," she said.

Joseph said, "I *feel* different."

Mary nodded. "You look—younger," she said.

Joseph looked at Mary. "As a matter of fact," he said, "so do you."

After that their lives changed.

What have Joseph and Mary discovered?

What should they do? Suppose they keep their "secret." What will happen? What will happen if they share their secret?

How will this story end? Will the world be a better place? Will Joseph and Mary get rich? Will someone steal the tree? Will Joseph cut the tree down?

What will your readers learn from this experience?

STRUCTURE AND STYLE

Connections: Selecting Verbs

As we noted in Strategies, the dividing line in "The Inheritance" is *After that his life changed*. The first part of the story is about a lonely man and his feelings. The second part of the story is about a social man, about language, thought, effort, and teaching. Merwin relies on a small number of verbs to carry out these two parts of his story: verbs of sense and verbs of comprehension.

1. Verbs of sense
We humans have at least five senses. The main ones are *sight*, *hearing*, *touch*, *taste*, and *smell*.

Which of these senses does Merwin use as he develops his story of the shepherd and book? Underline all the verbs of sense that you find in the first part of the story.

Which verb of sense is used most?

In what order does Merwin present the verbs of sense? Which one comes first? Which second? Which third?

2. Verbs of comprehension
To comprehend something is the act of trying to understand it, to know it. There are many ways that we comprehend things, and the list of verbs of comprehension is quite large. It would include verbs like *discuss*, *explain*, *think*, *discover*, *remember*, *teach*, *learn*, and so on.

Which verbs of comprehension does Merwin use as he develops the second part of "The Inheritance?" Underline all the verbs of comprehension.

Does comprehension lead to understanding and knowledge in "The Inheritance?" How do you know?

LAST WORDS

There was a time in the history of the English language when most people were illiterate: about 1,000 years ago. Only a few people — priests and scholars — could read and write. The rest of the population could only speak, listen to, and understand English.

Suppose you could choose whether to be illiterate — speak, listen to, and understand English — or to be literate: only read and write English, but not speak, listen to and understand spoken English. Which choice would you make? Why?

22
AT THE
PUBLIC
LIBRARY

William Saroyan

HEAD NOTES

See page 49.

CULTURAL NOTES

"At the Public Library" is from William Saroyan's novel, *The Human Comedy*, which is about the lives of ordinary people. The setting for the novel is a small town in California—a town like Fresno, where Saroyan spent much of his life.

Lionel and Ulysses are not part of the main action of the novel. They provide some amusement in a novel that contains sorrow and sadness because it is about the Second World War.

Saroyan shows a special skill when he writes about children and shows us the world from their point of view. Lionel is several years older than Ulysses, who is four years old. Lionel has never learned to read because his brain doesn't work very well. Ulysses hasn't learned to read because he is too young. The two boys are friends because of their lack of reading skill and their similar emotions. Notice that Lionel does all the talking. Ulysses doesn't say a word.

STRATEGIES

"At the Public Library" has a very simple plot: two young boys enter the library; they walk around and look; they answer the librarian's questions; they examine a book; and they leave the library. These events are ordinary. Our interest in the experience is focused on the characters—the two boys and the librarian.

Let these questions guide you as you read Saroyan's prose.

Why did the two boys visit the library?

Why do Lionel's answers surprise the librarian?

What is Lionel trying to explain to Ulysses?

What is Lionel unable to show Ulysses?

At the Public Library

William Saroyan

1   When the two boys entered this *humble but impressive* building, they entered an area of *profound* and almost frightening silence. It seemed as if even the walls had become speechless, and the floor and the tables, as if silence had *engulfed* everything in the building. There were old men reading newspapers. There were town philosophers. There were high school boys and girls doing research, but everyone was hushed, because they were seeking wisdom. They were near books. They were trying to find out. Lionel not only whispered, he *moved on tiptoe*. Lionel whispered because he *was under the impression* that it was *out of respect* for books, not consideration for readers. Ulysses followed him, also on tiptoe, and they explored the library, each finding many treasures, Lionel—books, and Ulysses—people. Lionel didn't read books and he hadn't come to the public library to get any for himself. He just liked to see them—the thousands of them. He pointed out a whole row of *shelved books* to his friend and then he whispered, "All of these—and these. And these. Here's a red one. All these. There's a green one. All these."

2   Finally, Mrs. Gallagher, the old librarian, noticed the two boys and went over to them. She didn't whisper, however. She *spoke right out*, as if she were not in the public library at all. This *shocked* Lionel and made a few people look up from the pages of their books.

3   "What are you looking for, boy?" Mrs. Gallagher said to Lionel.

4   "Books," Lionel whispered softly.

5   "What books are you looking for?" the librarian said.

6   "All of them," Lionel said.

---

humble but impressive—ordinary but important
profound—deep; great
engulfed—completely surrounded
moved on tiptoe—walked very quietly
was under the impression—believed
out of respect—because of admiration
shelved books—books on shelves
spoke right out—spoke loudly
shocked—surprised; upset

7 "All of them?" the librarian said. "What do you mean? You can't *borrow* more than four books on one *card*.

8 "I don't want to borrow any of them," Lionel said.

9 "Well, what in the world do you want with them?" the librarian said.

10 "I just want to look at them," Lionel said.

11 "Look at them?" the librarian said. "That is not what the public library is for. You can look into them, you can look at the pictures in them, but what in the world do you want to look at the outsides of them for?"

12 "I like to," Lionel whispered. "Can't I?"

13 "Well," the librarian said, "there's no law against it." She looked at Ulysses. "And who's this?" she said.

14 "This here's Ulysses," Lionel said. "He can't read."

15 "Can you?" the librarian said to Lionel.

16 "No," Lionel said, "but he can't either. That's why we're friends. He's the only man I know who can't read."

17 The old librarian looked at the two friends a moment and in her mind said something which very nearly approached a kind of *delicious cursing*. This was something *brand new* in all the years of her experience at the public library. "Well," she said at last, "perhaps it's just as well that you can't read. I can read. I have been reading books for the past sixty years, and I can't see *as how* it's made any great difference. Run along now and look at the books as you please."

18 "Yes, ma'am," Lionel said.

19 The two friends moved off into still greater *realms* of mystery and adventure. Lionel pointed out more books to Ulysses. "These," he said. "And those over there. And these. All books, Ulysses." He stopped a moment to think. "I wonder what they say in all these books." He pointed out a whole vast area of them, five shelves full of them. "All these," he

---

borrow—use briefly and return
card—library card: for borrowing books
delicious cursing—pleasant kind of swearing
brand new—completely new
as how—(informal usage) that
realms—regions; parts

said — "I wonder what they say." Finally he discovered a book that looked very pretty from the outside. Its cover was green, like fresh grass. "And this one," he said, "this one is pretty, Ulysses."

20   A little frightened at what he was doing, Lionel lifted the book out of the shelf, held it in his hands a moment and then opened it. "There, Ulysses!" he said. "A book! There it is! See? They're saying something in here." Now he pointed to something in the print of the book. "There's an 'A'," he said. "That's an 'A' right there. There's another letter of some sort. I don't know what that one is. Every letter's different, Ulysses, and every word's different." He sighed and looked around at all the books. "I don't think I'll ever learn to read," he said, "but I sure would like to know what they're saying in there. Now here's a picture," he said. "Here's a picture of a girl. See her? Pretty, isn't she?" He turned many pages of the book and said, "See it? More letters and words, straight through to the end of the book. This is the *pubalic liberry*, Ulysses," he said. "Books all over the place." He looked at the print of the book with a kind of *reverence*, whispering to himself as if he were trying to read. Then he shook his head. "You can't know what a book says, Ulysses, unless you can read, and I can't read," he said.

21   He closed the book slowly, put it back in its place, and together the two friends tiptoed out of the library. Outside, Ulysses *kicked up his heel* because he felt good, and because it seemed he had learned something new.

RETELLING

This story and the one preceding it, "The Inheritance," are both about literacy — writing and reading. Merwin's world is one that has lost literacy. In Saroyan's world of the two young boys, literacy is a skill that hasn't been learned yet. The library is a place of wonder and mystery — almost a place of worship.

Now that you've come to the end of *Experiences*, you have learned to read literature with greater skill and understanding. This is a good time for you to write down some of your thoughts. Here are some questions and suggestions to help you with your composition.

1. As possible titles, consider the following and decide which one is most agreeable.

---

pubalic liberry — Lionel's mispronunciation of "public library"
reverence — great respect
kicked up his heel — hopped and skipped with pleasure

a. Thoughts on Reading Literature

b. Opinions of (a) Writer(s)

c. What (the name of a writer or the names of two writers) Taught Me

2. Review the reading that you have done. Consider one of the following plans for your composition.

a. Select one story or poem because you especially liked it.

b. Choose two literary selections by the same writer (Lawrence, West, Kinnell, Saroyan, Hoppe, or Merwin). Compare or contrast the two selections.

c. Choose one literary selection that you liked and one that you disliked. They may be by the same writer or by different writers.

3. Plan to write at least three paragraphs on the topic of your choice.

a. In your first paragraph, present your choice of topics: the name(s) of the writer(s) and the name(s) of the selection(s). Next, give two or three reasons for choosing the poem(s) or prose selection(s).

b. In your next paragraph point out the specific features of the selection(s) that you found attractive and/or unattractive.

c. In your third (or final) paragraph, explain what you think the writer(s) taught you, whether it was attractive or unattractive to you.

STRUCTURE AND STYLE

Connections: A. Repetitions (Nouns and Verbs)

One of the secrets of Saroyan's style is his control of vocabulary. Saroyan limits his use of language, and he repeats a few key words many times.

To see how he does this, reread "At the Public Library" and count the occurrences of theses nouns: *library*, *book(s)*, *page(s)*, *letters*, *words*, and *pictures*. Which of these nouns does Saroyan use most often?

Now count the occurrences of these verbs: *read(ing)*, *look(-ed, -ing)*, + *at/into/for*, *see*, and *say(ing)*. Which of these verbs does Saroyan use most often?

If you could write only one sentence using the noun and the verb that Saroyan uses most often, what would your sentence say?

B. Substitutions (Pronouns)

If Saroyan repeated the same nouns too often, his style would become childish and tiresome. Therefore, Saroyan substitutes pronouns.

What are the words and phrases that Saroyan substitutes for *books*? How many substitutions did you find?

"At the Public Library" contains approximately 850 words. How many of these words are *books* and the pronouns for *books*?

How important is the repetition of key nouns (or pronouns) and verbs in Saroyan's style?

LAST WORDS

There are only three characters in Saroyan's little story: Lionel; Mrs. Gallagher, the librarian; and Ulysses. Two of them express opinions. What is Lionel's opinion of books? What is Mrs. Gallagher's opinion of books? Is there anything strange about her opinion?

Ulysses doesn't speak, but at the end of the story, Ulysses "felt good, . . . because it seemed he had learned something new." What do you think that Ulysses had learned?

ANSWER KEY

To complete *Retelling* successfully, you must find those words that make sense in two ways: their meaning must be appropriate and their grammar must be correct. Sometimes you will find the words you need in the reading (text) itself. Sometimes you will choose the right word from your own vocabulary—from words that you already know. Either way will work, if the words make sense in the context provided.

1. REFLECTIONS ON THE IGUANA
Isak Dinesen

RETELLING

The shape/appearance/look of the iguana, Isak Dinesen tells us, is ugly/not pretty, but its coloring is beautiful. The colors of the iguana's skin remind her of jewels/precious stones, or of a comet's tail, because they all shine.

After shooting/killing an iguana, she learned/discovered something that she never forgot. The live iguana was faded/fading and lost all of its color/life.

Isak Dinesen had a similar experience when she bought a bracelet from a Native girl. When Isak Dinesen put it on her own/white arm, the colors faded/disappeared, and it looked cheap/dead.

Isak Dinesen discovered the value of living things and dead things in a foreign country. Her advice to European settlers/people in East Africa is never to shoot/kill the iguana.

2. TO CHRIST OUR LORD
Galway Kinnell

RETELLING

Early on Christmas day/dawn/morning, a boy went out on snowshoes. He carried a gun/rifle. He heard the sound of wings/flying in the air, and he fired. He killed a bird. A woman cooked the bird for Christmas dinner. Someone said grace/prayers, and the boy wondered why he had killed/shot the bird. He had not wanted to shoot. He felt love/something stir inside him. But he fired his gun/rifle, anyway. When he saw the bird on his plate he ate it with wonder. There was nothing he could do but surrender/give in. Later, he went to the snow field and wondered/thought again. For whom had love stirred? The answer to his question was nothing. The stars above him glittered/shone in the sky.

3. REFLECTIONS ON THE DEATH OF A PORCUPINE
D. H. Lawrence

RETELLING

At the opening/beginning of his story "Reflections on the Death of a Porcupine," D. H. Lawrence and Madame/his wife were living on a ranch in New Mexico. Madame, Lawrence's wife, sees a porcupine and calls her husband. Lawrence asks his wife if he should kill the animal. When she says yes, Lawrence returns-/goes back to the house and gets a small gun/rifle. He has never shot any living thing in his entire life. Guns are disgusting to him. Nevertheless, he shoots the porcupine, but the shot/bullet doesn't kill it. Lawrence has to finish the job with a wooden/cedar pole.

This experience changed Lawrence's attitude toward killing animals. He used to hate/fear guns. Now he says, "One must kill." There is another porcupine on his property. Lawrence says that he must kill/shoot that one, too.

Lawrence now believes/thinks that man must fight against the lower orders of life, because every living creature needs food. A man must protect his crop with a gun. Every creature eats/devours the lower forms of life. Horses and cows eat grass and flowers. Chickens eat beetles. This constant struggle for food relates man with the animal and vegetable world.

4. SNAKE
D. H. Lawrence

RETELLING

In Sicily, there are two kinds of snakes: black snakes are innocent, but gold(en) snakes are poisonous/venomous. And the snake in this poem is described as earth brown (colored) because it lives in the bowels/interior of the earth. It drinks from a water/stone trough while the man waits/watches. As he waits/stands there, the man has a conflict inside himself. Should he kill the snake, as his education taught him? Or should he like/admire the beauty of the snake? He feels honored/pleased by the snake's visit.

The man compares the snake first to a human being and then to a god from the underworld/past.

After the snake finishes drinking, it begins to crawl/draw/climb back into the hole/fissure/crack from which it came/entered. The man throws/tosses a log at it, and the snake moves/goes/leaves quickly. Afterwards, the man regrets his action. He dislikes himself. He wishes that the snake would return, because it seems to be a king/god in exile. The man blames his education for his mean/stupid/cowardly act.

5. IN THE TREE HOUSE AT NIGHT
James Dickey

RETELLING

James Dickey's poem "In the Tree House at Night" is about three brothers. Two are living/alive and one is dead. The dead brother believed that they should build a tree house. However, the dead brother did not build it. The poet built it. He nailed steps on the tree trunk. He and his live brother are/lie together in the tree house. But the dead brother is also there/present. He is a spirit. He is not missing. He lives in the thoughts/trunk and the feelings/branches of the living/tree. The poet asks who is dead and whose presence is living. Can two bodies make up a third? The poet tells us that a house must be dead to be still. But this house moves, and it is filled with life. So in the end, we may ask/wonder, "Who *really* built the tree house?" "Is love/spirit stronger than death?"

6. THE PARSLEY GARDEN
William Saroyan

RETELLING

Al Condraj collected/gathered things and put them in an apple box. This is where he kept his junk. Al has saved/collected some nails from Foley's Packing House. He needed a hammer so that he could build/make something.

He saw/found the hammer he needed/wanted at Woolworth's. He put it into the pocket of his overalls. He stole the hammer, and he got caught.

Al told the store manager that he didn't mean to steal the hammer. He didn't have any money. That was not a good excuse/reason.

The store manager let Al go because Al promised never to steal from that store again.

Al felt bad/humiliated and guilty/ashamed. He hated both of the men in Woolworth's. He wanted to return to the store and steal the hammer again. This time he wouldn't get caught. But he couldn't enter the store, and finally he walked away. He felt crushed and confused.

When he got home he sat for awhile in the parsley garden. Then he told his mother what had happened at the store. His mother offered him ten cents so that he could buy the hammer. But he refused.

During the next day, while his mother was working at a fruit packing house, Al went/returned to Woolworth's. He worked all day, and he earned/made a dollar. The boss/manager offered him a job, but Al didn't accept his offer. Al also refused the dollar they offered him. Instead, Al took the hammer and went home.

Al's mother was pleased/happy with Al's work, but she wondered why he didn't take the money/job. Al told her that he hated both of the men at Woolworth's. He came home and made a bench. Al didn't feel humiliated/ashamed any more, but he still hated the two men.

7. THE DEATH OF THE HIRED MAN
Robert Frost

RETELLING

Warren, the farmer, and Mary, his wife, have an argument about Silas, the hired man. Mary likes Silas, and she wants him to stay. Warren will not hire Silas again, because Silas is old; and Silas leaves when he is needed. Silas returns in winter. Warren says, "I'm done." He means he's finished (with Silas).

Mary has sorrow/pity for Silas because he is worn-out/sick. She tells Warren that Silas has changed. But Silas won't tell Mary anything. He says that he will ditch the meadow for Warren, and clear the pasture, too.

Silas has met Harold Wilson, a boy who worked for Warren for several years. Silas wants to hay/work with Harold again, but Harold is now a teacher. Silas says that between them they will succeed. Silas wants another chance to teach Harold how to pitch hay. He hates to see Harold a fool. This means that he's sorry for Harold. Warren is sorry for Silas because Silas can't look backward with pride or look forward with hope. Mary tells Warren that Silas has come home to die. Warren mocks her. They disagree about the meaning of home. Warren says, "Home is the place where, when you have to go there, they have to take you in." Mary says, "I should have called it something you somehow haven't to deserve." These two statements show how different they are from one another.

Warren asks about Silas' brother, who is rich. Why doesn't he claim his brother for kin? Mary knows why: Silas is proud and won't be made ashamed. Mary asks Warren to be kind to Silas and not to laugh at him. Silas has come back with a plan to help Warren.

Warren goes to see Silas, and he returns very soon. Mary says, "Warren?" and Warren answers, "Dead."

8. THE MAN WITH THE HOE
Edwin Markham

RETELLING

Edwin Markham's poem, "The Man with the Hoe" was created/composed/written after he saw a picture/painting by the French painter Millet. This picture/painting shows a French peasant/farmer who looks like an animal/ox. This man's misery/condition/appearance made Markham angry/upset, and his poem expresses/tells his feelings/anger about this poor man's fate/misery/condition. Markham sees man in God's image. But the man in the painting is a "dread shape."

Markham blames/hates the "masters, lords and rulers in all lands" for this "monstrous thing." He asks what they will do to give back this man's lost hopes/life dreams. Markham believes that revolution/rebellion will come to the world in the future because of the wrongs/evil done to "The Man with the Hoe."

9. THE CORRESPONDENCE SCHOOL INSTRUCTOR SAYS GOODBYE TO HIS POETRY STUDENTS
Galway Kinnell

RETELLING

The correspondence school's instructor receives poems from all kinds of people/writers. They write about varieties of experience/things: a doctor/urologist from Miami wrote "Clinical Sonnets"; a manufacturer on the Coast wrote poems about sagging breasts; and a lady from Bangor/Maine didn't write poems at all: she sent snapshots of herself.

The instructor is bored by his job/work, but he is amused, too. He has read all their work/poems and has tried to tell them the truth about their writing/poems.

He is relieved/glad that it is over/finished. At the end, he has only pity for his students' work/poems. He says that their writing/poems keep smothering/killing life in words. These writers/people have become postmarks for him—not people. He is glad to leave.

10. A VALEDICTION: FORBIDDING MOURNING
John Donne

RETELLING

Usually, when lovers love each other, it is a time of joy/passion. Donne speaks of this kind of love as physical/earthly/sublunary love. In his valediction/poem to his lover/wife, Donne describes their love as refined/spiritual, and says that their two souls are one. Therefore their farewell/parting is not a breach but an expansion. Donne uses the metaphor of the compass to describe their two souls/lives. There is a fixed foot and a running foot. One remains fixed while the other moves. Donne describes his wife/lover as the fixed foot, while he is the running foot. It is the firmness of his wife's love that brings him home.

11. MOTHER AND SON
Liam O'Flaherty

RETELLING

Stephen Gill was nine years old, and he was a wild boy. He was an/one hour late coming home from school, and his mother was waiting for him. Stephen was her only child, and she had strong/mixed feelings as/while she waited for him. She was angry, but she was also anxious. Finally, she made herself think/believe that she was angry at Stephen.

When Stephen entered the yard of his house, he was worried/frightened. He knew that his mother would be angry because he was late. When Stephen entered the house, his mother grabbed/seized him. Stephen held his mother and began to shake/tremble. His mother couldn't whip/strike him, and instead she held/kissed him and began to tremble/cry herself.

She put/pushed him into a chair, and Stephen began to eat. Later she asked him why he had been so late. He told her that he had been playing ball with some other boys. A farmer named Michael chased them out of his field. Stephen ran/climbed over places/crags where he had never been before.

Stephen saw something on the crags. He made his mother promise not to tell his father what he saw. Finally, she agreed/promised, and Stephen told her about a big/black horse with seven tails and three heads and a big belly. None of the other boys saw what Stephen saw/did.

Stephen's mother was pleased by his story, and they sat together listening to the birds sing(ing).

12. CRESS DELAHANTY: SPRING
Jessamyn West

RETELLING

Cress Delahanty's first memory is about a time that she lied to a five year old boy named Tommy Fitzgerald. They were discussing/comparing the quality/price of hats, and Cress felt sorry for Tommy because his mother's hat was cheap. Cress lied because she liked Tommy.

Cress's next memory is of Hubert Fairchild who was five years older than Cress. Cress loved Hubert because he had been ill/sick with typhoid. Cress wished that she had been able to nurse Hubert when he had been sick/ill. She explains that sickness and suffering hadn't made her unhappy. It was Hubert.

Now Cress wants to suggest things to boys. She sits in assembly with her arm on the back of the seat next to her. She sits close to her father in his car so that people will think her father is a date/boyfriend.

But her real love is Mr. Cornelius, who is married, with three sons, and is thirty eight years old: older than Cress's father. Mr. Cornelius is dying/ill. He walks/moves with difficulty and he watches everything very intently.

Cress has spoken to Mr. Cornelius only once, but she thinks he knows that she loves him. He has a special look for Cress—of lovingness/tenderness. She feels that she understands him better than anyone else. He has more to leave behind than other people have, because he was an athlete. It is hard for him to leave the things of the world. Cress wants to suffer whatever he suffers, and most of all, she wants to save him or to make him happy.

13. CRESS DELAHANTY: WINTER
Jessamyn West

Cress Delahanty was away at school when she got/received a telephone call from her father. Cress heard/learned that her grandfather was dying. At first, she was angry/annoyed. She had never really liked her grandfather, and she disliked the idea of going home to watch him die. She decided not to go, because she couldn't do him any good. But her boyfriend/friend, Edwin, changed her mind, and they drove/went to the station. Cress went home on the train. The trip took about an hour and a half.

Cress and her father argued about her coming home. Cress's mother was suffering/haggard and told Cress that she might not see her grandfather again. Cress agreed to put/rub some medicine/ointment on her grandfather's throat and chest, to ease/help his pain/suffering.

As Cress rubbed in the ointment/medicine, she felt sleepy, but the old man woke her up by touching the bunch of flowers/violets that Cress was wearing. He spoke of Cress's grandmother, and he held the flowers/violets against his face. He spoke/said one more name, and closed his eyes.

Cress burst into tears, because in that moment, she knew that she and her grandfather were very much alike. Edwin had been right when he told Cress that her grandfather might do her some good.

14. HARLEM
Langston Hughes

I'll tell you what happens
When a dream is deferred
It dries up like a raisin
In the sun
It becomes festered/rotten like a sore
And it stinks like rotten meat
Or it crusts over
Like a syrupy sweet
Maybe we sag
Under its load
But one day
The dream will explode!

15. FEAST
Eric Larsen

RETELLING

When he was in the sixth grade, the narrator/writer remembers a special/particular day when his teacher planned to bring some Eskimos to visit the school/class. On the morning of that day it began to snow. By afternoon, the students and their teacher realized that the Eskimos/visitors would be late. The students read about Eskimos in their books, and the teacher told them once again about Eskimo women, who chew animal skins/hides to make them soft.

Later in the day, it began to snow heavily, but the teacher gave the students a recess, so that they could play in the snow. The girls played quiet games, but the boys' games were noisy/violent. One of the boys got a bloody nose.

Finally, the teacher called the students, and they went to the classroom. Inside they found/saw one Eskimo, a tiny woman dressed in leggings and a fur parka. The teacher showed the Eskimo woman how to open her mouth and show her teeth. Then the students walked/filed past the Eskimo and looked inside her mouth. Her teeth were almost gone/missing. She seemed to be afraid of the students.

Afterwards the students ran to the waiting buses that would take them home.

16. TULARECITO
John Steinbeck

RETELLING

Tularecito, which means Little Frog in Spanish, is the story/name of a boy/child who was found in the bushes by a hired/farm man/worker named Pancho. Tularecito is a very ugly boy, with a small head, short arms and long legs. As he gets/grows older/up, his brain/mind remains simple/childish, although his body becomes very strong/powerful, like that of a grown man.

Tularecito smiles a lot, and he is a peaceful/happy person. He has a talent/gift: he can make things out of clay, and he can draw pictures of all kinds of animals. Tularecito's pictures/drawings are very beautiful, and if people spoil/erase anything he has made/drawn, he gets/becomes very angry and hits/strikes them.

When Miss Morgan comes to teach in the school, she knows about Tularecito, and she asks/encourages him to draw/make pictures/drawings of animals. Miss Morgan is popular with the other students because she reads stories to them every afternoon/day. Tularecito doesn't pay attention to these stories/lessons until Miss Morgan begins to read fairy stories to the class. Then he listens very carefully when she reads about gnomes.

One day, as Miss Morgan is going/walking home from school, she meets Tularecito on a deserted road, and she is upset/frightened, because she doesn't understand/know what Tularecito wants. He wants/needs to talk about gnomes. He says that he knows them, although he has never seen them. Miss Morgan tells/advises Tularecito to look/search for gnomes/them at night, because they come out/appear only in the night/darkness.

Tularecito is happy, because he believes/thinks that he has found his own people who live in the ground/earth. At last, he is going home to be with them. Tularecito digs a deep hole at the foot of a peach tree in Bert Munroe's orchard. Bert Munroe sees/finds the hole and covers/fills it up again. He asks his son, Manny, about the hole, because he suspects/thinks that Manny has made/dug it.

Tularecito thinks that the gnomes have covered/filled the hole, because they were frightened. So Tularecito digs a new one/hole that is bigger/deeper than the first one. Then he retires and watches in the brush near the orchard. When Bert Munroe sees/finds the new hole, he starts/begins to cover/fill it with dirt. Tularecito hits Bert Munroe with a shovel.

When Jimmie, Bert Munroe's son, finds his father, he thinks that someone has tried to kill him, and Jimmie summons/gathers a group/band of men/neighbors to help him. Six men attack/grab Tularecito. They hit/strike him with a shovel and take him to jail.

At the examination/meeting in Salinas, a group of doctors asks Tularecito questions, but he will/does not answer them. The doctors decide that Tularecito is crazy/dangerous and that he may succeed in killing someone. Therefore, they send/commit Tularecito to the asylum at Napa.

17. THE FILIPINO AND THE DRUNKARD
William Saroyan

RETELLING

A.

As Saroyan tells us at the beginning/opening of the story, the guy/man "wasn't really mean, he was drunk." He disliked/bothered the young Filipino for that reason. The drunkard didn't really mean/want to hurt the Filipino. He pushed the Filipino and shouted/swore at him. Maybe the drunkard envied the Filipino, too. He told the Filipino that he was well-dressed, but he was only a dish washer.

The drunkard was a soldier/veteran in the war, and he was wounded. He is a white man and a veteran but nobody cares about him. He is a patriot/veteran, and he is angry/drunk. He wanted to frighten the Filipino, but he didn't want to hurt him.

The Filipino got frightened and ran away from the drunkard. The drunkard thought the Filipino was cowardly/frightened and pursued/followed him. The Filipino moved quickly and hid to avoid/escape the "drunkard." This was foolish-/wrong. He should have stayed in the crowd. He could have gotten help from someone. He never asked for help. But he stabbed the drunkard instead, and then he shouted/yelled at the people/crowd because they didn't/hadn't do/done anything.

B.

Saroyan tells us that the "loud-mouthed guy wasn't really mean, he was drunk." After reading the story, I think that Saroyan's "drunkard" hated the Filipino because

222

he wasn't white. The "drunkard" was really a racist. When he was drunk he was able to show/express his true feelings.

The "drunkard" was acting/making like/quite a bully/racist commotion. He pushed the Filipino and shouted/swore at him. The "drunkard" wanted to order/keep the Filipino around/down. The Filipino kept moving and hid in the lavatory because he was frightened.

Why did the "drunkard" bother/push the Filipino? Because he wanted to control/dominate him. Why did the "drunkard" shout/swear at the Filipino? Because he wanted to humiliate him. Was the drunkard successful?

If the Filipino had done nothing, the "drunkard" would have been successful. But the Filipino got/became angry, and his bitterness grew to rage. If the "drunkard" hadn't tried to keep the Filipino from getting/coming away/out, nothing would have happened. But the "drunkard" was a racist, and the Filipino killed/stabbed him. He didn't mean/want to kill/stab the "drunkard" but he had/saw no other choice. The people/crowd wouldn't help him.